Pavement Ends

*Mystery, History and Scenery
in Southeast Missouri*

James Baughn

Pavement Ends
Mystery, History and Scenery in Southeast Missouri

Copyright © 2024 by James Baughn

ISBN: 978-0-9745843-4-8

Published by:
Concord Publishing House, Inc.
Cape Girardeau, Missouri USA 63701

Dedication

This book is dedicated to the loving memory of James Owen Stanley Baughn (12/30/1980 – 12/06/2020). These are his writings, ramblings and musings about his hiking adventures in Southeast Missouri. Nearly every weekend or holiday found him discovering new places to explore and hike. He shared these adventures through his Southeast Missourian blog, *Pavement Ends*.

Unfortunately, his pavement ended way too soon during a hike. But we are left to fondly remember and can still trace his path through life with these reflections.

Happy Trails to our son.

Pavement Ends

Scenic Wonders

MYSTERY SPOTS

The Block Hole

Artificial mountain stream

Can you guess where this photo was taken?

Is it a mountain stream in Colorado? An Ozark shut-ins?

Nope.

It's the Block Hole in Cape Girardeau County, a man-made flood control structure along the Diversion Channel. Water diverted from Castor River tumbles over a series of rocks and into a large hole.

The Missouri Department of Conservation leases 10 acres to provide a boat ramp and public fishing access to the Block Hole and Diversion Channel. Even if you don't have any interest in fishing, this is still a unique place to visit, featuring a cascading stream and large boulders to scramble across.

If you squint your eyes, you can almost pretend this is a clear, rushing mountain stream. But the whole scene is artificial. The Diversion Channel is a man-made river designed to capture water from Castor River, Crooked Creek, Whitewater River, Hubble Creek, and other tributaries, and send the water directly to the Mississippi River. This keeps the water from overflowing into the flat lands of "Swampeast Missouri."

The problem with the Diversion Channel, however, is that it allowed water to move in the other direction when the Mississippi River was at a high river stage. A wall of blocks, called a weir, was constructed 11 miles upstream from the Mississippi to prevent river water from backing up too far along the channel. The weir

Water flowing over the weir carves out a large, circular basin at the Block Hole along the Diversion Channel.

also prevented the upper portion of the Diversion Channel from eroding down to the level of the Mississippi.

Water flowing through the channel has created this circular basin.

Over time, the water flowing over the weir carved out a large, circular basin – the Block Hole. That's what we have today.

In 2003, the U.S. Army Corps of Engineers performed extensive work to stabilize the area, bringing in large quantities of rip rap. The following year, the Conservation Department built a boat ramp and parking lot.

Directions

1. From Cape, take Highway 74 west to Dutchtown and turn left at the stoplight.
2. Follow Highway 25 to Delta.
3. Turn right on Route N and continue until you reach the intersection with Route U and T (the so-called "NUT Junction").
4. Make a right on Route U and look for the Block Hole Access sign and parking lot on the right.

Cupola Pond

Swamp at the top of a mountain

Cupola Pond in Ripley County might be one of the most bizarre natural places in Missouri. Somehow, a piece of "Swampeast Missouri" has been transplanted into the Ozark Mountains.

This small pond is filled with tupelo gum trees, usually only associated with swampland in the Missouri Bootheel or in the Deep South. It's an alien environment for the tupelo, sitting at an elevation of 800 feet above sea level, much higher than the level of the lowlands.

So how did the trees get here? It's a mystery. Researchers found that the sediment at the bottom of the pond is 23,000 years old, and they believe that the tupelos were here for most of that time.

Cupola Pond sits in a sinkhole, formed when the roof of a limestone cave collapsed, creating a round basin. So, it provides a nice habitat for the estimated 500 tupelo trees that stand here. But that still doesn't explain how the trees could cover the 40-mile distance from the tupelo's native habitat in the swamps near Poplar Bluff.

The pond's water level varies throughout the year. When I visited, the open water covered only a small area, while the rest of Cupola Pond featured a carpet of mud and old leaves. It didn't look safe to walk across at first, but the ground was (mostly) firm when I carefully tested it.

A trail forms a loop around the pond, allowing a close-up look at the tupelo trees without getting your feet wet, and without getting caught in a bunch of weeds. While difficult to reach,

Cupola Pond is one of the crown jewels of the Missouri Ozarks and an excellent place to visit if you like bizarre mysteries.

Directions

Brace yourself: these driving directions are even more difficult than usual.

1. Take your favorite route to Van Buren. The fastest route is I-55 south to Sikeston and then west on US 60, but Highway 34 through Marble Hill and Piedmont is more scenic.
2. Continue on Highway 60 past Van Buren, enjoying the four-lane highway.
3. Turn left on Route J before reaching Fremont.
4. Here's the hard part: you want to go south on Route J for 13.9 miles and turn left on Forest Road 3224. This turnoff is very difficult to find; don't feel bad if you miss it. You'll want to keep a sharp lookout after passing the junction with Route K to Wilderness.
5. Take FR 3224 east for 1.3 miles. At about the 1-mile mark, you will cross into Ripley County, where the road widens but the gravel gets rougher (at least when I visited).
6. When the road curves sharply to the right, look for the turnoff on the left for Forest Road 4822 (also called County Road C-7AB). This probably won't be marked.
7. Follow this gravel lane for nearly 2 miles until it abruptly ends at the Cupola Pond trailhead. This is a decent road suitable for passenger cars in good weather, but it certainly is narrow and might be a bit scary if this is your first "Pavement Ends" trip.
8. From the parking area, it's only a short distance along the trail to the pond.

Warning: Some information shows Cupola Pond in the wrong location, an error that thwarted my first attempt to find this place.

Gum trees align with Cupola Pond in Ripley County. Their haunting grandeur adds to the sense of mystery here.

Lithium

Once the smallest village in the country

The 2000 census declared that the Village of Lithium had a population of zero.

The hamlet has several houses, an old storefront, and, according to Google Maps, five named streets: Ladie Road, Blue Springs Lane, Williams Street, Cross Street, and St. Marys Street.

So how could it possibly have zero people?

Well, it depends on how you define "village." Most people would look at the cluster of houses and say, "There it is." Indeed, that's what the highway department did when they planted a "Lithium" sign along Route M.

The Census Bureau begged to differ. For reasons that are unclear, they considered the incorporated village of Lithium to only include a tiny parcel of land that is approximately 1.23 acres in size. That's only 0.001924 square miles or a little over 53,000 square feet. By comparison, a football field (with end zones) is 57,600 square feet.

Among all incorporated municipalities surveyed by the 2000 Census, Lithium easily had the smallest land area.

This wasn't always the case. The 1980 Census listed a population of 81 with a larger incorporated area. The Lithium quadrangle map from the U.S. Geological Survey shows the larger village limits.

So why did the corporate limits of Lithium shrink so much between 1980 and 2000? I have no idea. It doesn't make any

The 2000 Census Bureau proclaimed Lithium had a population of zero, even though it was clearly populated.

sense. Nevertheless, since no residents happened to live within this 1.23-acre sliver of land in 2000, the Census Bureau was technically correct in proclaiming that Lithium had a population of zero.

Lithium presented an interesting Catch-22 legal dilemma. According to an Associated Press story from March 2001, at least one resident would have to file a petition to formally dissolve the village under Missouri law. But there was nobody who could do that!

Thankfully, that is no longer a problem. The 2010 census restored the village's boundaries to their earlier size. Now the village officially has 89 residents. The downside, of course, is that Lithium can no longer boast that it is the smallest village in the United States.

History of Lithium

The village is worth visiting simply to see the Lithium Spring.

Charles F. Lawrence founded the town in 1882, hoping to take advantage of the medicinal properties of the lithium carbonate that flowed from the spring. At the time, some doctors prescribed lithium salts as a treatment for a variety of illnesses, ranging from gout to depression to mania, and even as a hangover cure.

The doctors were partially right. Lithium is indeed an effective treatment for the manic phase of bipolar disorder and might be useful for other ailments. But it didn't live up to the wild claims made by marketers in the late 1800s and early 1900s.

Mr. Lawrence's dreams of establishing a major health resort around the Lithium Spring fizzled, but the small town continued to grow. It was incorporated in 1883 and had a post office by 1884. A map from 1920 shows Lithium as a way point along the Cape Girardeau Northern Railroad between Perryville and Chester, Illinois. The rail line, bankrolled by Louis Houck, was never very successful and quickly became obsolete in the early 1920s with the coming of paved highways.

Despite losing the railroad and later the post office (discontinued in 1957), the village's population has held mostly steady, regardless of what the Census Bureau claimed.

Directions

From Cape Girardeau, take I-55 north to the Brewer exit (number 135). Take Route M east to US 61, turn right, and then turn left in Brewer to continue on Route M. Follow the road for almost five miles until you reach Lithium.

To get to the spring, turn right on Perry County Road 922 and follow the road as it zigzags left and then right through town. PCR 922 reaches PCR 921 at a T-junction; the Lithium springhouse is on the left.

Lithium is near other Perry County curiosities, including Falls Branch waterfall, Ball Mill Resurgence, the ghost town of Point Rest, and the crazy roadcut on Perry County Road 650 outside of St. Mary.

Artesian Wells of Bollinger County

Missouri is well-known for the 3 H's of summer: Heat, Haze, and Humidity.

When it comes to beating the heat, an artesian well is just the ticket. Bollinger County has two artesian wells accessible to the public. Thanks to a generous water table, these two sites – originally drilled as test pits for oil and mineral exploration – provide a permanent source of cold water.

An artesian well, according to Wikipedia, takes advantage of underground pressure to cause water to gush to the surface through a man-made tap. The name is derived from the Artois region of France.

Woodland Artesian Well

The most well-known of Bollinger County's artesian wells sits next to Woodland School, just west of Marble Hill.

It generates a steady stream of water that flows into Crooked Creek.

Look for the gravel pullout along Highway 34 and the peculiar "No Parking 8 Feet of Pavement" sign (I think it means "No parking within 8 feet of the pavement"). A path leads south to the wellhead.

Not as well known, but just as impressive, is the "Sycamore Valley" artesian well on National Forest land near the Madison County line.

Sycamore Valley artesian well pumping water in a fantastic display, characteristic of its behavior.

Sycamore Valley Artesian Well

It sits just off County Road 872, gushing water down the hillside and across the road.

When I visited during a summer's drought, the artesian well was still pumping plenty of water. The surrounding area had a spongy, muddy feel, almost like the ground was sweating. According to one source, the Sycamore Valley well, with a depth of 1,300 feet, produces an average of 50 gallons per minute.

Both sites are an excellent place to visit on a sweltering day. It's hard not to get wet.

Directions

Woodland School Artesian Well: From Cape Girardeau, take Highway 34 west through Jackson and Marble Hill. Outside of Marble Hill, drive just past Woodland School and look for the gravel pullout on the left as the highway starts to curve. The well can be seen from the pullout.

Sycamore Valley Artesian Well: From Cape Girardeau, take Highway 72 west through Jackson and Millersville to Patton Junction. Turn left on Highway 51, drive through Patton, and then veer right at the intersection with Route A. Then turn right on Route O at the intersection. After one mile, turn left on County Road 872. The well is just shy of two miles down this road, on the left.

Schnurbusch Karst Window

It's a window. On karst.

Missouri is called The Cave State, and for good reason. The ground under parts of Missouri resembles Swiss cheese, riddled with caves, sinkholes, springs, and other curiosities.

This kind of landscape is called "karst topography." It forms when the bedrock, usually limestone or dolomite, partially dissolves, leaving subterranean voids. Perry County, Missouri, is the King of Karst, with over 650 known caves, a number that continues to increase as spelunkers make more discoveries.

While none of the Perry County caves are open to the general public, the karst world can still be glimpsed from the surface. Take, for example, the "Schnurbusch Karst Window" on the grounds of St. Joseph Catholic Church in the village of Apple Creek, northwest of Old Appleton.

This is the site of a collapsed cave. Water emerges from a spring...

...and then flows under a stately stone bridge...

...before being swallowed into the ground again.

The church has taken advantage of the topography to create a peaceful park, complete with benches forming an amphitheater. It's only a short walk from the parking lot, making it a cool place to visit during the dog days of August.

Schnurbusch Karst Window is open to the public, but you may have to come back later if you visit when the church is holding services or special events here.

The Schnurbusch Karst Window offers a fascinating glimpse of a subterranean river as it briefly breaks the surface.

Directions

1. Take I-55 north to the Old Appleton exit, turn right on Route KK, and then left on Highway 61. You can also take Highway 61 directly to Old Appleton from Fruitland.
2. Follow Highway 61 north to Uniontown and turn left on Route F.
3. After two miles, turn right on County Road 520.
4. Follow CR 520 a short distance to the cross and parking lot next to St. Joseph Catholic Church (on the left). Park here and walk down the trail, passing the Stations of the Cross, until you reach the Karst Window.

Ball Mill Resurgence

Long before humans invented indoor plumbing, the Earth had its own plumbing systems consisting of caves (pipes), sinkholes (drains) and springs (faucets).

With any plumbing system, things don't always go smoothly. In Cape Girardeau, we're familiar with the downtown storm drains that back up when the Mississippi is above flood stage and start to leak water on Water Street.

Nature has similar plumbing problems. Take, for instance, Ball Mill Resurgence in Perry County. Most of the time, Ball Mill is just a sinkhole, draining surface water that falls into it.

During wet weather, however, enough water pressure builds underground to turn the sinkhole into a spring. It surges water, flooding the banks of a creek bed that is usually dry.

The sinkhole/spring is at the bottom of a circular depression, flanked on one side by a tall bluff.

Following a heavy rain, rocks trapped in the bottom of the depression are bounced around by the gushing water, creating a natural rock tumbler. The "mill" action of the water has created a nice collection of smooth, round "ball" rocks. It's an odd sight for Missouri. To see naturally polished rocks, you usually need to go to a Colorado mountain stream.

A sinkhole and spring flanked by a tall bluff. Views like this one are rare in Southeast Missouri.

Hiking directions

Designated as a State Natural Area, Ball Mill is a short hike along a loop trail. The first portion of the trail passes a cultivated field dotted with obvious sinkholes.

At the fork in the trail, take the left branch. The trail meanders around a series of sinkholes that are uphill from the main Ball Mill sinkhole.

One of the sinkholes is choked with fallen trees from storm damage (Ice Storm 2008, Ice Storm 2009, or Inland Hurricane 2009, it's hard to say which).

The trail then drops to the bottom of the hill, rounds a corner, and crosses the creek below the Ball Mill.

On the way back to the trailhead, the trail re-climbs the hill, following an intermittent stream and series of small waterfalls.

Directions

From Cape Girardeau, take I-55 north to the Perryville exit (#129). Turn right and take Highway 51 to the stoplight at US 61. Turn left on US 61, go north 1 mile, and turn right on Route V. Follow Route V until the highway ends at a fork. Take the right fork (County Road 916) and continue 1.5 miles to the Ball Mill Resurgence parking area on the left.

The Gulf

Want to visit a giant hole in the ground?

Wayne County features a massive sinkhole and underground lake known as the Blue Hole. It's also called "The Gulf," an accurate name for the deep void that opens to the surface.

This isn't the kind of destination that you would want to spend all day driving to. However, if you're already heading to Clearwater Lake, Current River, or somewhere else in the Ozarks, then this site south of Piedmont is a nice little diversion.

When you first pull into the parking area, you're greeted by an ominous chain-link fence to prevent people and animals from accidentally wandering into the hole. After entering the gate, it's only a few feet to the rim of the sinkhole. The rim is 40 feet above the surface of the water below. Watch your step!

What you can't see is even larger. According to the book Geologic Wonders and Curiosities of Missouri, the Blue Hole opens into a cave that extends for another 500 feet beneath the hillside. The water is even deeper within the cave, with divers exploring the underground lake to a depth of 200 feet.

For the adventurous, a difficult path leads down into the sinkhole and the edge of the water. Anything beyond that will require a boat and caving equipment.

A massive sinkhole called "The Gulf" for the deep void that opens to the surface.

Directions

1. Take Highway 34 west to Piedmont, a distance of roughly 75 miles from Cape Girardeau.
2. In Piedmont, follow Highway 34/49 south for 7 miles, and then turn left where Highway 49 branches off.
3. Drive 2 miles south to Mill Spring and make a right (following Highway 49) at the stop sign in town.
4. Go another 2 miles and look for the turnoff for Carson Hill Cemetery Road on the right. Follow this gravel road up and over the hill for roughly two miles.
5. Keep your eyes peeled for Blue Hole Road on the right. If you reach a low-water bridge, you've gone too far. Blue Hole Road is a rough gravel road, but it's only a short distance to the parking lot.

The Fish Trap

In this book, I showcase Lee Bluff in Madison County as one of the best panoramic views in Missouri. The view from below isn't too shabby either.

This valley along the St. Francis River is the kind of place that is worth visiting in every season.

This photo was taken from a spot colorfully known as The Fish Trap. A natural dam juts into the river, creating an obstruction that forces the water to flow around.

The dam is covered in potholes that collect and hold water when the river level rises and falls. It's not hard to imagine that unlucky fish would find themselves trapped in these pockets following a flash flood.

If any fish do get trapped, they wouldn't last long, as the area is patrolled by bald eagles and other aerial attack avians.

We may never know which pioneer or mapmaker came up with the name, but The Fish Trap was an appropriate choice. This landmark is the centerpiece of a long stretch of the river filled with rocky ledges and cascades.

Just like Lee Bluff, it may be hard to believe that this is part of Missouri. But that's fine. The tourist hordes can continue to invade Colorado or West Virginia while we Missourians keep these little natural wonders to ourselves.

A water hole called The Fish Trap made from a natural dam. It lives up to its name and then some.

Directions

The Fish Trap is reached from the same Forest Service road as Lee Bluff.

From Cape Girardeau, take Highway 72 West through Jackson and Patton to Fredericktown. Follow the Highway 72 bypass around Fredericktown. At the roundabout, take the second turn to stay on Highway 72 West. Go straight through the stoplight and then turn left for the US 67 South onramp. Follow the freeway a short distance to the next exit for Route E.

Turn right on Route E and drive 5.3 miles to Route O. Turn left on Route O and follow this road for almost 5 miles until the pavement ends. Continue straight on County Road 425. After crossing a low-water bridge, the road forks. Bear right on County Road 408. After driving past a farm, the road becomes narrower and rougher.

Keep going for a quarter-mile beyond the last house and look for an ATV trail on the left. This is the trailhead for Lee Bluff, discussed previously. The main road continues straight ahead to The Fish Trap. Depending on your comfort level, you have the choice of parking here and hiking along the rest of the road, or driving all the way to the end (high clearance vehicle recommended).

Either way, the road meanders for another mile, going up and over a ridge, before ending at a campsite just before a creek. The Rock Pile Mountain quadrangle map shows this location as Bill Smith Hollow.

A faint quarter-mile trail leads south to the Fish Trap. This trail, however, is hard to find at first. From the end of the road, walk downstream (to the left) along the edge of the creek to a small but picturesque shut-ins.

Beyond this point, the creek forks into two channels. Here the trail should be easier to spot as it crosses one branch of the creek to an island, and then back again (if the water is too deep, it may be necessary to bushwhack through the woods above the creek before rejoining the trail). Follow the rest of the trail to the St. Francis River and The Fish Trap itself.

Cape Girardeau County Road 532

Try exploring County Road 532. It meets CR 535 about halfway between Neelys Landing and Route CC, just north of the bridge over Lovejoy Creek. It runs southwest and eventually reaches Pocahontas. At first, this looks like another gravel road. But the sign that says "IMPASSABLE DURING HIGH WATER" is not kidding.

This part of the road, if you can call it a road, drops into Lovejoy Creek and stays within the creek bed for nearly three-quarters of a mile. Nature provided a flat-bottomed gravel creek, and the county has taken advantage of this natural roadbed. But I wouldn't want to be here in low water, much less high water.

The photos don't do this place justice. This is not a road, it's a creek, with steep banks on either side and a driving surface consisting of large, uneven rocks.

It's not for the faint of heart. But where else can you drive down the middle of a creek without trespassing?

For a real adventure, drive on this dry creek bed that pretends to be a road.

Seventy-Six

Perry County has several towns that once thrived thanks to the Mississippi River, but have since vanished thanks to the river's relentless flooding. Claryville, Belgique, Point Rest, Menfro, Red Rock Landing, Seventy-Six, Star Landing, and Wittenberg are all towns that have either vanished or dwindled to a mere shell of their former selves.

The ghost town of Seventy-Six, located north of Altenburg and Frohna, has been lost to the encroaching river. The town site was acquired by the Conservation Department in 1990. What was once a bustling river landing is now a secluded area featuring a rocky creek, quarries, sinkholes, river overlooks, and armadillos.

Cline's Branch, a boulder-lined creek, runs parallel to the entrance road before emptying into the Mississippi River.

Above the creek, a hiking trail leads past a series of "diggings" where limestone rock was quarried. The rock face stands 10-20 feet above the abandoned quarry sites.

Drill holes can still be seen in the rocks. One outcrop was drilled completely through.

Some of the exposed rocks feature a hodgepodge of fossil fragments. The cylindrical pieces are portions of crinoids, the official Missouri state fossil.

Continuing past the quarries, the hiking trail soon reaches the top of a ridge with plowed fields.

The ridge provides a quality view of the river valley into Illinois.

A line of deep sinkholes straddles the edge of the fields. Some of the sinkholes have formed natural ponds.

Once a river, rock formations remain.

In Perry County, with its many cave systems, sinkholes are a dime a dozen. However, Seventy-Six is one of the few places in the county where sinkholes can be explored on public land.

Moss covers the inside of this crevice at the bottom of a sinkhole. This is where I spotted an armadillo peeking out of a hole.

Very little remains of the original town of Seventy-Six. The entrance road, County Road 437, crosses the railroad tracks and dead-ends at the river. This was once the site of several large buildings.

Many different explanations have been given for the origin of the town's peculiar name. The Ramsay Placename File says:

Three stories are told concerning the naming of the landing, which was known as Landing Seventy-six. According to one version: "In 1844 there was a great flood. The steamboat captain who had been sent to rescue the people reported that he made seventy-six landings. They also said prior to 1879 various men tried to keep the ferry landing and no one stayed long enough to give it a name, so the old steamboat captain's report was retained in "Landing Seventy-six." Another theory also concerns a steamboat captain (whether the same one or not legend does not reveal), "who had quit swearing and had acquired the habit of exclaiming, 'That beats all 76', when he was vexed. He used the expression so often at that landing the steamboat men had got in the habit of calling it Seventy-six." Still another theory persists, and it is the most logical one, that the Government River Commission numbered the river landings and this was No. 76 from the head of the navigable waters.

One story is that it received its name because it was the 76th boat landing after leaving St. Louis. Another is that the first man to land a boat at the location was celebrating his 76th birthday. Still, another story is that John Wilkinson, who was to later found the town, sank his boat on the river two miles up from the future town of Seventy-Six, Missouri, after previously making 75 successful landings. Legend has it that Mr. Wilkinson painted a board on the opposite bank "76 LDG," from which the town took its name.

Putting the theories together, it seems most likely that steamboat captain John Wilkinson chose the name, but it's hard to tell exactly what kind of 76 he had in mind.

The land on the opposite side of the river is called Wilkinson's Island. The course of the river shifted after the state lines were drawn, so this "island" is entirely within Missouri.

The Conservation Department has constructed a boat ramp at the Seventy-Six town site, making it possible to launch a boat from Missouri, cross the river, and land in Missouri on the opposite shore.

Directions

From Cape Girardeau, take I-55 to the Fruitland exit. Then take US 61 north through Fruitland to the turnoff for Route C. Turn right and follow Route C as it snakes through Pocahontas, New Wells, Altenburg, Frohna, and Brazeau. At Brazeau, turn right on Route D (look for the Seventy-Six Conservation Area sign). Follow Route D to where the pavement ends and continue straight ahead on Perry County Road 437 to enter the conservation area.

The trailhead for the main hiking trail is at the second parking area on the left. Be sure to print a copy of the Conservation Department map of the area.

Launch from Missouri and land in Missouri from this boat ramp at the former town of Seventy-Six.

Reynolds County Sinkhole

Warning: The location featured is more hazardous than the usual "Pavement Ends" destination. The edge of a growing sinkhole is not your friend.

In 2020, a massive sinkhole opened in Reynolds County, taking down a bunch of trees and swallowing a segment of the Trail of Tears.

Located south of Viburnum, this sinkhole developed, forcing the closure of Reynolds County Road 907 within the Mark Twain National Forest. The hole isn't quite large enough to span the length of a football field, but it's getting there. I measured a diameter of 180 feet while walking around the rim with a GPS receiver – and keeping a safe social distance from the abyss (and subtracting that distance from the total).

It's hard to imagine the commotion that must have occurred when the sinkhole first opened. If a sinkhole sinks when nobody is around, does it still make a sound?

The sinkhole sits between two lead mines: the Buick Mine (to the northeast) and the Brushy Creek Mine (to the southwest), both operated by The Doe Run Company. A ventilation shaft is located one-third of a mile to the south of the sinkhole.

Hopefully, this situation won't remain unresolved indefinitely. The gaping wound in the earth had forced the closure of a historically significant road.

The road traces the original path of the Hildebrand Route of the Trail of Tears. During the winter of 1838-39, Peter Hildebrand directed a large detachment of Cherokee through the Ozarks by sticking to the ridgelines where possible.

A massive sinkhole swallowed a segment of Trail of Tears in 2020 and remains unstable.

In 2013, signs were installed along 31.7 miles of the road. It was announced that this was the "longest marked original route trail segment on the Trail of Tears to date."

It will be interesting to see what happens next.

Directions

From Cape Girardeau or Jackson, take Highway 72 West through Fredericktown to Arcadia. After crossing the viaduct at Arcadia, make two right turns to stay on Highway 72. Continue to the junction with Highway 49 and veer right (west) toward Lesterville. A few miles after passing through Lesterville, turn right on Highway 49 (this junction is easy to miss).

After 5 miles, Highway 49 turns into Route J. Continue straight on Route J until it ends at Route KK. Turn left on Route KK and drive 1.2 miles. Then turn right on County Road 907 (shown as Karkaghne Scenic Drive or Forest Road 2352 on some maps). Look for the Trail of Tears signs.

Drive approximately 2 miles on this gravel road until you reach the barricade. Then walk – carefully – to the sinkhole a short distance ahead.

HISTORIC SITES

Old Appleton Bridge

It took almost 27 years, but the Old Appleton Bridge, one of the oldest bridges in Southeast Missouri, is now listed on the National Register of Historic Places.

According to an article in the old Bulletin Journal, paperwork for nominating the bridge had been completed as far back as 1982. However, for reasons that are not explained, the original nomination was never submitted. (Procrastination, perhaps?)

Then, on Dec. 3, 1982, heavy rains sent a flash flood down Apple Creek, pushing the bridge off its foundations. The surge of water left behind a crumpled wreck of girders in the pool below the mill dam.

Many towns would have immediately given up following such a disaster, but Old Appleton rallied to put the bridge back together. Little did they know that more setbacks were coming, holding back the bridge's restoration until 2005.

Another flash flood in 1986 wiped out the McClain Mill which once stood next to the bridge. The community pushed ahead with the bridge restoration, despite the huge void left by the missing mill.

By the 1990s, the wrought-iron girders for the bridge's main span had been re-assembled. The bridge was back together again, even if it didn't span anything but weeds.

After years of waiting, the stage was finally set in the Summer of 2005 to install the bridge back to its rightful place. Enough money had been raised from local donations and government grants to hire a contractor, A.E. Simpson Construction of Scott City, to finish the job.

First, the two smaller approach spans were lifted into place on top of the new-and-improved piers.

Then, a barge and crane were used to carefully hoist the main span into position on Sept. 23, 2005.

With a new paint job, the bridge looked better than new.

A formal dedication ceremony was held Apr. 22, 2006, including the obligatory ribbon cutting.

The celebration also included a parade of vintage cars. To preserve the bridge's longevity, it is only open to pedestrians and bicyclists. Although, as the parade demonstrated, it is more than capable of carrying light traffic.

It wasn't possible to save all of the original iron thrown into the water by the flash flood, but the vast majority of the bridge was constructed from authentic material. This isn't a re-creation of a lost bridge, it's the real thing. One spare girder was reused to support a birdhouse next to the bridge and mill site.

The plaques on the bridge proudly proclaim that it was constructed by H.W. Sebastian & Co. of St. Louis in 1879. Sebastian also built a similar, but slightly newer, bridge that still stands in Columbia, Mo. The company later became the St. Louis Bridge & Iron Co and built many bridges across Missouri, a handful of which still survive.

Old Appleton Bridge isn't the oldest iron bridge in the state (it's beat by the 1875 Windsor Harbor Bridge), but it is believed to be the oldest wrought-iron highway bridge still in its original location in Missouri.

In some ways, the Sebastian Co. was ahead of its time. The design is almost indistinguishable from other bridges built through the 1910s, except that Old Appleton employs wrought iron instead of steel, which became popular about 15 years later. Compare this 1879 bridge with one from 1915, and it might be hard to tell them apart.

Old Appleton Bridge is now listed on the National Register of Historic Places, and with good reason.

Based on its early construction date and ahead-of-the-curve design, the Old Appleton Bridge is the perfect addition to the National Register of Historic Places. It's nice to see that the damage from the 1982 flood has finally been undone.

Three Notch Road

Missouri has over 123,000 miles of public roads. We've come a long way since the very first road was blazed in the early 1700s.

Called the Three Notch Road, Missouri's first road connected the lead mines at Mine La Motte with the newborn town of Ste. Genevieve. The road, if you can call it that, was little more than a horse trail through the woods. It was so difficult to follow that travelers had to keep a sharp lookout for three notches etched into trees along the route.

This stretch of Perry County Road 840 follows the Three Notch Road.

The practice of notching trees continued into the early 1800s. According to one source, it was common to mark minor roads with one notch, secondary roads with two notches, and major roads with three notches.

The Dec. 20, 1940, edition of the Southeast Missourian includes this curious item: "E.B. Dickey, an employee of the state-wide highway planning survey, who is making a study of old roads and trails in the state, recently located several of these old notched trees in the northeastern part of Madison County, of which he has several pictures."

I don't know if any of those trees remain, but the original Three Notch Road is still mostly intact and drivable. The definitive history of the road was written by Milan James Kedro, who first retraced the route as part of a Boy Scout project. In a 1973 article, he wrote: "By traveling state highways and backroads in a southwesterly direction from Ste. Genevieve, it is possible to parallel rather accurately the path of the old trace."

Kedro's article, however, didn't give specific driving directions. He did mention that the road forded the South Fork of Saline Creek at the "Old Burnt Mill" in Perry County.

The ford was a convenient stopping point because it was roughly half-way between Mine La Motte and Ste. Genevieve. In the 1800s, a series of mills were built to take advantage of the current along Saline Creek. The largest mill, a massive four-story stone structure, was built in the 1850s. It burned during the night of Oct. 12, 1866, never to be rebuilt.

Even now, three of the walls remain standing, a bizarre scene for rural Perry County. The ruins are best viewed in the winter from the bridge on Perry County Road 840.

Falling trees and flash floods have taken their toll, but the mill ruins are still impressive. The whole thing looks pretty unstable, though, and will continue to crumble.

Southwest of the Burnt Mill ford, the Three Notch Road followed a high, narrow ridge that separated two deep hollows. This stretch was called "The Narrows" (or shortened to "The Nars").

From there, the road stuck to high ground when possible, skirting around the headwaters of Whitewater and Castor rivers. Naturally, early travelers wished to avoid muddy creek crossings as much as possible, even if meant climbing over difficult terrain.

At a place called Cross Roads, the road apparently intersected the Farmington-Jackson Road, a road that is still called "Old Jackson Road" in St. Francois County.

Approaching Mine La Motte, the road probably crossed Rock Creek near the Madison County line. The current bridge over Rock Creek, a small concrete structure from 1919, was one of the first bridges designed by the newly created Missouri State Highway Department.

The road's starting point at Mine La Motte is marked by a historic marker along Route OO (formerly US 61/67).

It says, "This tablet marks the site of the first lead mine opened in the Mississippi Valley about the year 1700. It is named for Antoine De LaMotte Cadillac, Governor of Louisiana, 1710-1717."

The lead mines played a key role in local history, providing a reason for people to venture to this side of the Mississippi River. The Three Notch Road made it possible to transport the valuable lead to the outside world, creating Missouri's first industry. While the road soon faded in importance thanks to other roads and railroads, it remains as a scenic byway and historic site.

Directions

To reach the Old Burnt Mill from Cape Girardeau:

Take I-55 north to the Brewer interchange (Exit 135). Turn right on Route M, then make a left on US 61. Bear left on Route NN. After 3½ miles, turn left on Perry County Road 840. Drive down the hill and look for the mill on the right while crossing the bridge.

To follow Three Notch Road:

Continue on CR 840 past the mill. At the intersection with CR 842, bear right up the hill. Follow CR 842 (also called Burnt Mill Road) until it ends at Route N. Turn left and continue on Route N until the pavement ends. Continue straight on Holmes Road. After a few miles, the road ends at Route WW. Turn left on Route WW, then turn right on Route T. Eventually, Route T will make a sharp right curve at the intersection with Old Jackson Road. Turn left here to join Old Jackson Road, then veer right on Rock Creek Road. At Route OO, turn left. The Mine La Motte historic marker is about one mile away on the right side of Route OO.

This 1850's mill was once a massive four-story stone structure.

Gads Hill

What about the really obscure towns, those that appear in Flyspeck-3 on maps (if they're lucky)? This book, of course, is all about obscure places to visit. So, with that in mind – and with a nod to April Fool's Day – I'm kicking off a new series called Not Your Town, profiling local wide spots in the road that have seen better days.

We start in Gads Hill, a hamlet along Highway 49 north of Piedmont in Wayne County. At its peak, this placename only had a handful of houses and businesses, and today it has even fewer.

The town's namesake is Gad's Hill in Kent, England, the setting for a highway robbery in Shakespeare's Henry IV Part I.

How fitting, then, that Gads Hill in Missouri (somehow losing the apostrophe) was the setting for another kind of robbery on Jan. 31, 1874. Jesse James and friends picked this location for the first train robbery in Missouri.

Gads Hill was the high point along the Iron Mountain Railroad between Des Arc and Piedmont. This made it the ideal spot for a hold-up.

In an article in Wild West Magazine, author Ronald H. Beights explains in detail how the robbery went down. Five masked men rode into Gads Hill and took control of the town and railroad station. They threw a switch so that the next train would be shunted to the siding and forced to stop. Then the robbers proceeded to... well, rob the passengers at gunpoint.

What was most ingenious about the robbery, however, wasn't the robbery. It was the public relations.

The gang handed one of the passengers a pre-written press release so that the newspapers would get their facts straight. Supposedly, it read:

THE MOST DARING ROBBERY ON RECORD

The south bound train on the Iron Mountain railroad was boarded here this evening by five heavily armed men and robbed of _ dollars. The robbers arrived at the station a few minutes before the arrival of the train and arrested the agent and put him under a guard and then threw the train on the switch.

The robbers were all large men, none of them under six feet tall. They were all masked and started in a southerly direction after they had robbed the express. They were all mounted on fine blooded horses. There's a hell of an excitement in this part of the country.

Of course, the press release took some liberties with the truth. The gang rode northwest, not south, after the hold-up. Not that anybody would expect the gang to broadcast their real destination to the authorities. The phrase "hell of an excitement" was correct, however, as word spread to newspapers across the country and Gads Hill became the focal point of a national media frenzy. The robbery elevated Jesse James to the level of celebrity.

The James gang tried to position itself as a modern-day band of Robin Hoods, stealing from rich, lazy capitalists while sparing women, children, and hardworking men. At the beginning of the hold-up, the robbers announced they would uphold this principle, but by the end it was clear that they were willing to steal from anybody. The Jesse-James-as-Robin-Hood myth, however, took hold at Gads Hill.

Today, a historic marker along Highway 49 is the only remnant from that fateful day in 1874. The Iron Mountain Railroad – now Union Pacific – is still in operation, but the line was altered after World War II to accommodate higher-speed trains. It now

This sign marks Jesse James' first train robbery in Missouri.

cruises through Gads Hill on a higher grade and jumps over Highway 49 at a concrete overpass.

Even the name Gads Hill was almost lost to history. The town and post office changed to "Zeitonia" from 1887 to 1906 before reverting back to Gads Hill. The post office remained in operation, off and on, before shutting down for good in 1940.

Directions

To reach Gads Hill, take Highway 34 west from Cape Girardeau all the way to Piedmont. At the intersection with Highway 49, continue straight on Highway 49 North, crossing the viaduct over the railroad tracks. Continue on 49 for roughly six miles and look for the Jesse James historic marker on the right, in front of a tavern.

Missouri Mines

For sale, cheap. Slightly used lead mine with 8,000 acres of land. Comes complete with original equipment, tailing piles, and EPA regulations. Buy now or be priced out forever!

That describes the situation in the 1970s when the St. Joe Minerals Corp. shut down its Federal Mine on the outskirts of Flat River (now Park Hills). The lead ore at the "Lead Belt" had played out, to be replaced by new mines to the southwest at Viburnum.

In the end, the company donated the old mining complex and surrounding land to the state of Missouri, eventually creating St. Joe State Park and Missouri Mines State Historic Site. The historic site occupies the hulking remains of the Federal Mine No. 3 just off the Highway 32 bypass of Park Hills.

One source described the mine and milling operation as "the largest plant of its type in the world."

Many of the buildings remain, although much of the complex is roped off for safety reasons. However, it's possible to explore some of the grounds and peek inside the buildings.

No mill would be complete without a "crusher building" and "headframe" (whatever that is).

Or a "floatation plant" (another fine example of mining jargon).

The old powerhouse has been converted into a museum, featuring exhibits showcasing the Lead Belt as well as mining history throughout Missouri. You'll have to visit the museum to learn the purpose behind the headframe, floatation plant, "Dorr Thickener Tanks" and other structures.

An old mining works, once a thriving complex, now a Missouri Mines State Historic Site.

From the parking lot, a trail leads south into the surrounding St. Joe State Park, with 8,000 acres of old mine tailings and sand flats suitable for hiking, horseback riding, and off-road vehicles.

Meanwhile, to the north, one of Park Hill's infamous chat piles can be seen in the distance.

The pile, composed of mine waste, is currently undergoing work to stabilize the whole structure to prevent lead and who-knows-what-else from affecting nearby residential areas. Local residents are not entirely thrilled about how this will change Park Hill's skyline.

Directions

From the US 67/Highway 32 interchange at Park Hills, go west on the Highway 32 bypass to the first exit, turn left, and follow the signs.

Birds Point Highway

It may seem hard to believe, but Mississippi County, Missouri, has been a leader in civil engineering projects. The Charleston area has been home to three "firsts" in Southeast Missouri: the first railroad (Cairo & Fulton Railroad), the first major concrete highway (the Charleston-Birds Point road), and the first stretch of completed interstate (a short segment of I-57).

The railroad is long gone and the interstate isn't that interesting. However, the old concrete highway is quite an amazing sight, featuring pavement that is almost 100 years old and yet remains in surprisingly good condition.

Other stretches aren't quite as nice, with many patches and cracks, but are still decent.

For something constructed in 1919-1921, I think the engineers and construction crews would be quite proud that their work has held up so well. If only our modern roads could be built with such longevity!

These first roads were designed in an era where cars had a top speed of 35 mph or less. This road only has a width of 16 feet with many sharp curves.

It also crosses a narrow bridge with a wooden floor. A plaque states this bridge was constructed in 1921.

It didn't take long for this road to become obsolete as people wanted to drive faster. By 1938, most of the route was bypassed by a new and improved highway. A map from the 1930s shows both roads in operation at the same time northeast of Wyatt.

The route marked "60" was the new highway, while "62" marked the old, zigzagging road. Since then, most of the old highway has been relegated to county roads used only by locals.

The book *History of Mississippi County Missouri: Beginning Through 1972* by Betty Powell offers this description of the highway project:

The first project inaugurated, known as 7-A, consisted of 15 1/2 miles of sixteen-foot concrete pavement on the state road from Charleston to Bird's Point. A letting was held for the project on Oct. 1, 1919, with Roy L. Williams, Wyatt, being the low bidder, the contract price being $507,777.30. Clyde Swank was an engineer for the project. The contractor installed equipment consisting of a steam shovel, a large mixer and an industrial railway plant to haul stone, sand, and cement to the work. The road was completed in November of 1921, it could transfer traffic to Cairo, Illinois. It was the first stretch of concrete highway in Missouri other than a three-mile road between Kansas City and Independence, Missouri.

That road at Kansas City has probably been paved over numerous times, leaving the Charleston road as the oldest concrete highway in Missouri still carrying traffic. That may seem like an obscure achievement, but similar historic roads in Arkansas have been posted to the National Register of Historic Places. I don't see why the Charleston road couldn't also qualify.

I found more references to this project in the Southeast Missourian "Out of the Past" archives.

From Apr. 26, 1920:

One of final steps in work preliminary to construction of Charleston-Birds-Point concrete road was accomplished Saturday when construction of industrial railway which will transport materials from Missouri Pacific tracks was completed into Charleston; railway is about two miles in length, being built from material

The oldest concrete highway in Missouri still carrying traffic. It is in remarkably good shape for its age.

switch put in on Cairo Branch, about one mile east of city limits, to Sixth street in Charleston, at which street construction of road is to begin.

From May 20, 1921:

Julien Friant, Eugene Hart and representative of this newspaper drive to Charleston to see new concrete road that is being built from Charleston to Bird's Point, opposite Cairo; nearly nine miles of road have been built and are now in use; crushed stone, sand and cement are unloaded from cars on side track short distance east of Charleston and dump cars are then loaded with correct mixture of each; motorcar hauls a train of dump cars out over road to point where new road is being laid, where it is dumped into mixer and spread out on road by machinery.

It appears this was quite an undertaking, requiring the construction of a special railroad line. As the first project of its kind in Southeast Missouri, the construction process would have been quite a spectacle.

Directions

Located only a short distance east of Charleston, the old highway is a perfect scenic diversion to accompany the Dogwood-Azalea Festival in the spring.

This Google map shows the exact route of the highway, starting in Charleston and working its way in zigzag fashion to Birds Point:

Here are the directions for retracing the highway:

1. The road started at the intersection of Sixth Street and E. Marshall Street (US 62, the main drag) in Charleston.
2. If you take I-57 to Exit 12 (the US 60/62 exit), you can pick up the road on the east side of Charleston. Turn right (east).

This highway follows the original road, but there's no original pavement left here.

3. Turn right (south) on Route JJ. The original road would have made a sharp turn here.

4. Turn left (east) on County Road 340. Soon you'll come to the original concrete pavement, 16 feet wide. This road is straight as an arrow until it suddenly veers left just before Highway 77. Follow the paved road into Wyatt and follow Main Street diagonally through town.

5. Main Street crosses Route EE (on the levee) before turning into Route HH. Continue straight on Route HH – this road sits on the original concrete roadbed but has been resurfaced numerous times.

6. Make a left on County Road 307. This is the best part, with the original concrete pavement appearing again. The road curves right and then left on a pair of sharp corners.

7. CR 307 continues north and crosses the 1921 steel truss bridge.

8. Beyond the bridge, notice the gap in the concrete pavement where the big levee was constructed. Cross over US 60/62 and continue straight ahead on County Road 205. This is still the original road, but has been resurfaced.

9. The road intersects with Route K and zigzags to the right and left. Before reaching US 60/62 again, the old road veers left and follows a dead-end route to the river. This is where a ferry crossing to Cairo would have operated before the Mississippi River Bridge was completed in 1929.

10. Turn right on US 60/62 to return to Charleston on the "new" highway built in the 1930s.

Belmont

The town of Belmont, in Mississippi County southeast of Charleston, is served by its own paved state highway. Too bad nobody lives there.

Belmont, once an important river landing and the home to a Civil War battle, isn't even shown on most modern maps. It's easy to find, though. Take I-55 south to Highway 80, turn east, and keep going until the pavement ends. You'll come to a dead-end sign, a rare sight for a major state highway.

A few miles later, I'd recommend stopping at the stop sign. It means business: The water's edge is only a few feet beyond the sign.

Throughout most of its history, Belmont has had a ferry boat connecting to Columbus, Kentucky. The ferry is long gone, but the highways on either side – both numbered Highway 80 – still remain.

If the ferry was still operating, it would be possible to enter Kentucky and follow the highway across the entire length of the state and into Virginia. Indeed, Highway 80 is the longest state highway in Kentucky, providing a continuous connection – minus the ferry – between Missouri and Virginia.

Belmont dates to 1853 when a river landing was established and named for August Belmont, a wealthy and powerful New York banker. It remained a sleepy hamlet said to contain "three shacks." That changed during the Civil War.

Across the river at Columbus, the Confederates built a fortification on top of the bluffs. Confederate Maj. Gen. Leonidas Polk called his fort the "Gibraltar of the West." He knew that control of the Mississippi River was a vital part of the war for both sides. In order to stop the passage of Union supply ships, a giant chain was stretched across the water from Columbus to Belmont.

Attacking Columbus directly would have been foolish for the Union, especially since it was the home to 140 cannon. The biggest was the "Lady Polk," a cannon capable of shooting 128-pound projectiles and reported to be the largest operated by the Confederacy at the time.

Brig. Gen. Ulysses S. Grant decided to attack the Confederates on the opposite side of the river, at a small camp they had erected at Belmont. This was the Battle of Belmont on Nov. 7, 1861. By Civil War standards, it was fairly small, but it was still deadly.

The battle was inconclusive. Grant took the Confederate camp, only to be forced to retreat as enemy reinforcements arrived. Indeed, Grant barely escaped to a departing riverboat ahead of a surge of Confederate soldiers.

Despite the battle's relative unimportance, it does have one claim to fame: it was U.S. Grant's first experience commanding a large force in combat. It helped pave the way for his rise through the ranks. History might have been very different if Grant had been unable to escape from Belmont.

Even after the war, Belmont and Columbus continued to occupy a strategic point along the river. Now it was the railroad tycoons who came calling. In 1869, the Iron Mountain Railroad constructed a branch line, the Belmont Branch, to the river landing. Several towns were platted along the line, including Allenville and Glenallen, named for the railroad's head tycoon, Thomas Allen of St. Louis.

On the other side of the river, the Mobile & Ohio Railroad provided connections to the Deep South. With the Belmont Branch in place, St. Louis had direct access to the Gulf.

Belmont enjoyed the railroad boom until bridges were built at Cairo and then Thebes, diverting rail traffic through Illinois

A giant chain stretched across the water to stop Union army ships, at a town that no longer exists.

instead of Missouri. The town declined until floods in the 1920s finished the job for good.

Today, Belmont offers little except a Civil War historic marker and access to the water. It's an interesting place to visit, but would hardly be considered a tourist attraction.

Bloomfield Road

One of the most storied roads in Southeast Missouri, the Bloomfield Road has provided a connection between Cape Girardeau and Bloomfield since the 1830s. It's gone through various incarnations: stagecoach route, military road during the Civil War, toll road, and state highway.

Today the original route is followed by a patchwork of county roads, city streets, and state highways. The whole thing can be driven from end to end, although a handful of detours are required where the original road is missing. Much of the road, especially along Crowley's Ridge in Stoddard County, remains fairly primitive. It provides a stark reminder of the challenging conditions that early motorists faced. Here is a detailed guide to retracing the old Bloomfield Road.

Cape Girardeau

During its days as a toll road, the so-called "Cape Girardeau-Bloomfield Gravel Road" started at the intersection of Sprigg and Good Hope streets in Cape. It made a jog in front of the old St. Francis Hospital site to reach Bloomfield Street. A tollhouse stood at the intersection with Koch Avenue.

Turning southwest, Bloomfield Road left town and soon intersected the Benton Road, another early road connecting the county seats of Jackson and Benton. Here was Mount Tabor, an early settlement featuring what has been described as the oldest American school west of the Mississippi, established in 1799.

Following the Ranney Creek valley, the road then encountered the "Big Swamp" separating Cape and Scott counties. It turned west, hugging the hills, to reach Dutchtown. The route was bypassed by a new concrete road, Highway 74, in 1930-31.

Directions

Take Bloomfield Road west from Cape Girardeau, then turn right at Highway 74. Continue west to Dutchtown.

Dutchtown

The road at Dutchtown has been rebuilt at least twice. Evidence of the earlier roads can be seen along Dutchtown Loop on the west side of town.

A short distance west of Dutchtown, the road forked, with the right fork heading to Whitewater and beyond. The Bloomfield Road followed the left fork, leading to Allenville.

Directions

At the stoplight in Dutchtown, continue straight on Route A. Where Route A forks at the "Allenville 4" sign, bear left on to County Road 241.

Allenville

Platted by the Iron Mountain Railroad in 1869, the town of Allenville was named for railroad tycoon Thomas Allen. A covered bridge was constructed to carry the Bloomfield Road across Whitewater River on the southern edge of town.

This historic bridge was destroyed by a windstorm in 1945.

The current bridge is no match for the original covered bridge.

After the Diversion Channel was built south of Allenville, the road had to be relocated. A massive iron bridge, originally built elsewhere over Whitewater, was relocated in 1918 to span the "Big Ditch." This bridge collapsed in 1977, leading to an ugly legal and political battle over building a replacement. Now that replacement bridge is starting to show its age.

It might be an optical illusion, but the current Allenville Bridge does seem to be sagging in the middle.

Directions

Follow CR 241 into Allenville, where it becomes Penney Street. Follow the street around the right curve and continue on Whitewater Street. At the T-junction, turn left on CR 238. Follow this road across two bridges to reach Route N.

Round Pond

The Bloomfield Road was an important route for moving soldiers and supplies during the Civil War. On Aug. 1, 1863, a Union wagon train stopped to camp at a place called Round Pond along the road. They were attacked that night by Confederate guerrillas. Sources vary as to the final death toll, but the scene was sufficiently bloody to earn the name "Round Pond Massacre."

The pond no longer exists, but the site is marked by a private lane called Old Round Pond Lane.

Directions

Turn right on Route N. Just before the Delta Elementary School, turn left on CR 254. Follow this road to the T-junction at CR 253 and turn left.

Hickory Ridge

In the 1800s, road builders tried to avoid swampy lowlands, so the road was built up and over the high ground of Hickory Ridge.

Hickory Ridge is completely surrounded by lowlands, however, and the road builders had no choice but to bring the road down into the swamps.

From a place called Rum Branch, the road traveled southwest, clipping through a corner of Bollinger County, before reaching Stoddard County near the villages of Toga and Lakeville.

The gravel surface changes color at the county line.

Directions:
Follow CR 253 to Route NN. Turn left on Route NN, then bear right on CR 278. This becomes Bollinger County Road 430 and then Stoddard County Road 203.

Toga and Lakeville

Lakeville, surrounded by lakes and swampy ground, was appropriately named.

When the Houck Railroad arrived in the 1880s, the tracks bypassed Lakeville to avoid the excessive land prices demanded by residents.

At the location where the Bloomfield Road crossed the railroad, a new settlement emerged called Toga, named for Toga Bill Rhodes. It seemed like an ideal choice for a new town. But it faced competition from another town founded a short distance to the southwest, strategically named New Lakeville. Toga lost the competition to the "advancing" town of New Lakeville. We now call New Lakeville, Advance.

The old settlements of Lakeville and Toga never completely died, and a cluster of houses remain at both town sites.

Driving through Toga

Directions

At the intersection with Highway 25, continue straight to go through Toga on CR 303. Make a left at the T with CR 310 and follow this road through Lakeville to Route O.

Tilman

From Lakeville, the road turns to the southeast to reach the drier ground on top of Crowleys Ridge. It reaches the town of

Tilman, still marked by a church and some houses. The place was named for landowner Squire John Tilman.

Beyond Tilman, the original road disappears from modern maps until it picks up again south of Highway 91.

Directions

Turn left on Route O, then make a right on CR 309. Follow this road until it ends at Route OO. Turn left on Route OO, go through Tilman, and continue to where the pavement ends. Bear right to continue on CR 337. Upon reaching Highway 91, turn right and then make a left on CR 331. Keep your eyes peeled for the right-hand turn for CR 317. This curvy road finally rejoins the original Bloomfield Road.

Castor River

The road followed the backbone of Crowleys Ridge. In some places, it clings to the highest point of the hill, flanked by surprisingly steep hollows on both sides. Elsewhere, the one-lane road cuts through hillsides, sandwiched between steep banks offering little clearance on either side.

Eventually, the road dropped to lower ground to cross Castor River. Here is another gap in the original road. An iron bridge was built in 1906 one mile to the east, so it appears, for whatever reason, that the route was shifted. That iron bridge still stands but is abandoned.

To overcome this gap, it is necessary to drive west to cross the Castor River on Highway 25 at Aquilla.

Directions

At the intersection with Route Y, turn right. Follow Route Y as it zigzags to Highway 25, then turn left. Take Highway 25 south through Aquilla and turn left on Route AB. Look for the turnoff for CR 525 on the right.

Bloomfield

After crossing the Castor, the road then resumed following the backbone of Crowley's Ridge. At the home stretch approaching Bloomfield, the road turned southwest to drop away from the ridge. It entered the town on Cape Road, a street that still exists. Naturally, it was silly for the Bloomfieldians (or Bloomfieldites?

Bloomfielders?) to call the road "Bloomfield Road." To them, it was the Cape Road.

Directions
Follow CR 525 until it merges into CR 510. Continue on CR 510, then make a right at the T-junction with CR 514. Turn left on Highway 25 to enter Bloomfield, then bear right on Cape Road.

Congratulations, you've made it to Bloomfield, hopefully without suffering any flat tires or getting caught after dark without headlights.

New Bourbon

Some time ago, construction began on a dollar-intensive project to build a "New Bourbon Port" along the Mississippi River in Ste. Genevieve County.

But where exactly is New Bourbon? What's the story behind the strange name?

The original town of New Bourbon was located a few miles south of Ste. Genevieve. Modern maps, if they show it at all, place New Bourbon just west of the intersection of Highway 61 and Bourbon Road.

Bourbon Road has the appearance of an ancient road, with a deep cut through the hill plus several sharp curves.

On the opposite side of Highway 61, Cottonwood Road runs to the northeast toward the river and the site of the future port. Lying in a floodplain, the area is mostly empty farmland.

It's hard to believe that this was the site of a bustling town. The Census of 1799 reveals that New Bourbon had a population of 560, slightly larger than Cape Girardeau with a population of 521. (These numbers probably include surrounding areas and not just the town proper.)

The story behind New Bourbon starts in France during the French Revolution. Following the storming of the Bastille in 1789, the French aristocracy realized that their days were numbered. Some fled to America, avoiding the guillotine that was soon to be used on King Louis XVI.

An outfit called the Scioto Company took advantage of the situation by offering land in Ohio to the French immigrants. The land was billed as a "Garden of Eden." When the French immigrants arrived in 1790, they discovered that they had been swindled. Ohio was not Eden, and the deeds they had purchased from the now-bankrupt Scioto Company were worthless.

Nevertheless, some of the immigrants remained in Ohio and were able to persuade the U.S. government to grant them land. Their settlement was called Gallipolis, a town that still exists on the banks of the Ohio River. Conditions, however, were terrible, with swampy land giving rise to disease.

This is where the story gets complicated. One of the Gallipolis immigrants, Pierre De Hault De Lassus De Luziere, came from a background of European nobility. He had been, according to one account, a member of the council of the King of France, and inherited an estate with an annual income of 30,000 crowns. I don't know what the crown-to-dollar exchange rate would be, but De Lassus was quite wealthy until the French Revolution ruined everything.

De Lassus had been childhood friends with Baron de Carondelet, the Lieutenant Governor of Upper Louisiana in 1793. At this time, Upper Louisiana – including modern-day Missouri and other states – was controlled by Spain.

The Spanish were on the lookout for "warm bodies" to settle in the territory and provide a buffer between the Americans on the east and the Osage Indians on the west. Carondelet hoped that De Lassus and other Gallipolis refugees could be some of these "warm bodies" and relocate to Louisiana.

Convincing an unhappy group of French bluebloods and urbanites to move to the edge of civilization wasn't easy. Carondelet set aside a chunk of land as their new home, calling it Nouvelle Bourbon (New Bourbon). This was a clever piece of propaganda, as "Bourbon" referred to the royal dynasty that had controlled both France and Spain. When King Louis XVI of France was beheaded on January 21, 1793, the royal bloodline was still alive

The Dellassus-Kern House is the only remnant of New Bourbon.

in Spain under the crown of King Charles IV. Carondelet figured that the French immigrants would be more at home under the Spanish monarchy rather than American democracy.

De Lassus moved with his family to New Bourbon, arriving in August 1793. However, it appears that none of the other Gallipolis residents made the journey west. Perhaps they were worried about getting swindled again, or maybe they had heard rumors about Missouri's heat and humidity.

The De Lassus family did well in Louisiana. Pierre was immediately appointed as the commandant of the Nouvelle Bourbon district (including the town plus the prosperous lead mines at Mine La Motte). His son, Carlos, would become the lieutenant governor of Upper Louisiana in 1799, a post he would hold until the Americans took over during the Louisiana Purchase.

New Bourbon grew during the 1790s as settlers moved into Upper Louisiana. Francois Valle built a mill near New Bourbon, described by one source as the "first mill west of the Mississippi," on what became Dodge's Creek.

In 1799, the residents of New Bourbon raised money to give to the King of Spain as a "patriotic war contribution." The total amount donated was 565 piastres, although I have no idea how much this would be in dollars. The list of donors is included in Louis Houck's History of Missouri and provides a detailed record of (most) of the people who lived there, featuring an eclectic mix of French, Spanish and American names.

After the Louisiana Purchase, New Bourbon declined as the town's population and importance were absorbed into nearby Ste. Genevieve. With the river port now under construction, the New Bourbon name will live on, even while the town is long gone.

Point Rest

The name Point Rest, found on maps of Perry County, definitely lives up to its name. It's very restful. In fact, there's absolutely nothing here except a levee and a couple of gravel roads.

Point Rest was never very big, but it did have a post office (from 1891-1940), a store, and a river landing. However, floods along the Mississippi, especially in 1927, took their toll on Point Rest and many other settlements in Perry County.

Many places along the river no longer exist: Marie, Grand Eddy, Killian, Wilkinson, Seventy-Six, Starland, Pit, and Gerler. Older maps from the late 1800s show even more placenames. Meanwhile, towns such as Wittenberg, Belgique, and Claryville were prosperous at one time but are hanging on by a thread today.

The flatland along the river opposite Chester, Illinois, is known as the Bois Brule Bottom, from the French phrase for "burned woods." Surrounded by tall hills on both sides, it's quite a scenic area.

When visiting in early April, the henbit was on full display in the fields. Henbit is a weed, but it's a pretty weed.

The Bois Brule Levee surrounds the area, protecting it from the Mississippi River and its tributaries, Cinque Hommes Creek and Bois Brule Creek. A gravel road runs the length of the levee, making for a nice drive on a sunny spring day.

At the southern end of the Bois Brule, damage was caused by a tornado in 2006 that ripped through Crosstown before heading across the Mississippi. The twister destroyed trees along entire hillsides.

Missouri and Illinois meet at this turn.

If you take the levee road to the north, toward Chester, you will suddenly enter into Illinois – without crossing a single bridge. A small piece of Illinois now sits on the Missouri side of the river at a place called Crains Island. The river shifted course since the state lines were surveyed, leaving a piece of Randolph County, Illinois, on the "wrong" side.

In this photo, the foreground is part of Missouri while the background is Illinois. At least, that's what the maps show – there's absolutely no indication of the border crossing from the road.

The topographic map of the area is quite strange. I'm not sure how a state line could have an "indefinite boundary" on dry land, but that's what happens here.

Similar border anomalies, known as "avulsions," can be found all along the Mississippi River, with the most well-known located at Kaskaskia, Illinois.

Directions

From Cape Girardeau, take Highway 61 north to Perryville. Just after reaching the city limits, turn right on Route E (Allens Landing Road) and follow it for several miles until you cross Bois Brule Creek and the railroad tracks. Here the road meets the levee, with the Bois Brule Bottom on the other side. You can explore in any direction – left, right, or straight – but I'd suggest turning right on the levee road (marked as County Road 354 here) and following it for as many miles as you want to drive. This will take you to Menfro, followed by the southern tip of the floodplain, and then back around to the north before reaching Point Rest (or what's left of it).

You can also reach the Bois Brule by taking Route C from Fruitland to Menfro via Altenburg. Highway 51 from Perryville toward Chester is another option, but not quite as interesting.

Fort Davidson

Historic markers at every corner

Drive through Arcadia Valley and it's hard to miss the red-granite blocks that are the construction material of choice for just about everything: buildings, footbridges, gates, and plenty of historic markers.

Occupying a strategic location during the Civil War, the Arcadia Valley saw more than its fair share of military action. The towns of Arcadia, Ironton and Pilot Knob are now filled with historic markers for every skirmish and event during the Civil War.

Why Arcadia?

Iron County experienced a boom just prior to the war thanks to its namesake: iron mining. Surveyors in the 1840s and 1850s believed that Pilot Knob Mountain and nearby Iron Mountain were composed of solid iron ore, with one source boasting that they "have enough material in their bowels to supply the world for a century." An estimate from 1859 suggested that Iron Mountain might be worth 5 billion dollars!

In order to tap into this bonanza, the St. Louis, Iron Mountain and Southern Railroad was chartered in 1851. The railroad reached Pilot Knob on April 2, 1858, but plans to continue building south were halted by the Civil War.

The "Iron Horse" brought prosperity to Iron County, but it also brought suffering during the Civil War. Thanks to the railroad terminus and mining industry, Arcadia Valley found itself in the cross hairs of both sides.

Fort Hill

After the Civil War officially started at Fort Sumter in April 1861, it wasn't long before the Union arrived on the scene at Arcadia Valley. A small fort, first called Fort Hovey but later renamed Fort Curtis, was established at a high point in Arcadia, providing a clear view of the valley and Pilot Knob.

Pilot Knob is easy to spot from the old fort.

The site of Fort Hovey/Fort Curtis, known today as "Fort Hill", is occupied by the Fort Hill Apostolic Church. No surprise, a historic marker can be found here.

Directions
Take Highway 72 west into Arcadia. Just after crossing the viaduct, make an immediate left on College Street, then a quick right on Church Street. Fort Hill is at the high point at the end of the street.

Iron County courthouse

It's not unusual to find historic markers at a courthouse square, but Ironton offers a bonus: original damage from a Civil War artillery shell. Completed just prior to the war, the courthouse withstood heavy back-and-forth fighting, but the facade was damaged by a Confederate artillery barrage into Ironton.

Grant Was Here. So Was Emerson.

A parcel of land just south of the Ironton courthouse played roles in the careers of two famous, but unrelated, people.

Ulysses S. Grant's military career had humble beginnings at Ironton, his first command as a brigadier general. He remained in Ironton for only 11 days in August 1861, but it was here that he received word that his appointment as brigadier general by Abraham Lincoln had been confirmed.

No surprise, a historic marker and statue marks the spot where he received the good news, although it's hard to tell if the statue is supposed to represent Grant or just a generic Union soldier.

Grant's headquarters was located on the lawn of John W. Emerson's home. After the war, Emerson gained fame as the namesake of Emerson Electric Company.

In 1890, he met brothers Alexander and Charles Meston, who were working on a patent for an electric motor. They convinced Emerson to invest $50,000 in start-up capital to get their invention off the ground. Emerson served as the first president of the company until he retired in 1892. With the successful introduction of the first electric fan, the company quickly expanded to other products. It is now a Fortune 500 company still based in Missouri.

Curiously, this is one of the only points of interest in Ironton that doesn't have its own historic marker.

Directions

The site of Grant's headquarters and Emerson's estate is now part of the grounds of Ste. Marie du Lac Catholic Church. From the intersection of Shepherd and Russell streets at the southwest corner of the courthouse square, take Shepherd Street south one block to the church parking lot and then walk over to the statue next to a picturesque lake.

Fort Davidson

Concerned that the Confederates in Arkansas may try to advance into Missouri, Fort Curtis was replaced by the more substantial

Fort Davidson at the foot of Pilot Knob. In September 1864, Confederate general Sterling Price raided into Missouri, hoping to capture St. Louis. He decided to attack Fort Davidson, leading to the Battle of Pilot Knob. Technically a Confederate victory, it was a costly battle for the South and forced Price to abandon his goal of attacking St. Louis.

The distinctive summit of Pilot Knob rises above the Fort Davidson visitor center.

The fort's hexagonal earthworks are still intact, except for the giant hole in the middle where the powder magazine was deliberately ignited by the retreating Union army.

Immanuel Lutheran Church

Located just a few blocks due north of Fort Davidson, the Immanuel Lutheran Church served as a Union hospital during the battle and possibly even as Union headquarters. Yet another red-granite historic marker tells the story.

Directions: From the Fort Davidson visitor center, take Ziegler Street four blocks north; the church is on the left just past Pine Street.

More historic markers

Fort Davidson State Historic Site publishes a driving tour giving directions to all of the historic markers in Arcadia Valley, including several more not mentioned here.

If you're visiting Fort Davidson or nearby Elephant Rocks, be sure to check out some of the other historic markers and sites in Arcadia Valley.

Fruitland

Southeast Missouri is filled with numerous mysteries involving placenames. Where did Seventy-Six in Perry County come from? How did a town without any marble get to be known as Marble Hill? Is Fredericktown named for George Frederick Bollinger, Frederick Bates, Frederick the Great, or some other guy named Fred? Why has everybody always pronounced New Madrid, Cairo, Vienna, and other names completely different than their Old-World counterparts?

The town of Fruitland poses another difficult problem. According to conventional wisdom, the name refers to a fruit orchard planted in the area. This idea is backed by the Ramsay Placename File compiled under the direction of Robert L. Ramsay at the University of Missouri. Mayme L. Hamlett, who researched Cape Girardeau County for the project in the 1930s, concluded that Fruitland "was named from the nursery for fruit trees established there by Edgar Wallace."

The grave of James Edgar Wallace at Pleasant Hill Cemetery

James Edgar Wallace, according to an obituary in the Southeast Missourian (Feb. 8, 1937), "spent most of his life near Fruitland, where he formerly operated a nursery." His death certificate lists an occupation of "Nurseryman - Retired."

Sounds good, right? Well, maybe. The study of placenames (toponymy) is rarely this easy. In a 2007 newspaper story about Fruitland, historian Dr. Frank Nickell mentioned that the name had nothing to do with fruit growers. "There were no orchards there," he said.

Another newspaper clipping, from 1949, supports this idea. Fruitland was "so named because early residents thought the high, rolling area would make good fruit-growing country, but no extensive orchards were ever planted."

While the origin of Fruitland is murky, we do know the origin of Pleasant Hill, the name that came before Fruitland. John Oliver, Sr., settled with his family on Indian Creek in the 1810s. He dubbed his estate Pleasant Gardens.

The "Pleasant" name carried over to Pleasant Hill Presbyterian Church and then Pleasant Hill Academy. Founded by John Oliver, Jr., the academy (under the umbrella of the Presbyterian church) was one of the first schools of higher learning in the area.

Meanwhile, the "Hill" in Pleasant Hill was a logical choice. The area occupied high ground at the headwaters for major creeks in all directions: Indian Creek to the east, Hubbell Creek to the south, Byrd Creek to the west (via Horrell Creek) and Apple Creek to the north (via Shawnee Creek).

Most atlas maps from the time of the Civil War until the 1880s clearly show Pleasant Hill as a village on the road between Jackson and Perryville. It was during this time – 1869, to be exact – that the name "Fruitland" was first used in the form of the "Fruitland Normal Institute."

This school was founded by Professor James Hutchinson Kerr, a Pennsylvania native. After graduating from Yale University in 1865, Kerr turned down a job as the Assistant Geologist of Mexico, instead opting to move to Cape Girardeau County. He was soon appointed as the first superintendent of the county public school system.

The public schools needed teachers, which meant that the region needed a school to train the teachers. That was the basis for the Fruitland Normal Institute, which Kerr hoped would eventually become a regional university. However, that plum went to Cape Girardeau in 1873 as the newly selected home for the Third District Normal School, now Southeast Missouri State University.

Dr. Joe P. Dunn, a professor at Converse College in South Carolina, prepared a book on the life of Professor Kerr. I expect this is an interesting biography, as Kerr sounds like quite the Renaissance man.

In a brief sketch for American National Biography Online, Dunn writes that Kerr "was a prolific author of letters to newspapers in which he advocated labor and women's rights, education reform, improved roads, opposition to capital punishment, and promotion of service to humanity; he also challenged the traditional religious thought and practices of the day."

Those were some heady political beliefs to hold in rural Cape Girardeau County in the years following the Civil War. As a transplanted Yankee, Professor Kerr probably stuck out like a sore thumb in this part of the country. Nevertheless, his career continued to blossom during the early 1870s. Dunn explains that "Kerr served simultaneously as county superintendent of schools, president of the county teachers association, vice president of the state teachers association, lecturer and curator of the state university, and organizer of more than two hundred teacher training institutes."

After contracting tuberculosis, Kerr decided to move to Colorado Springs in 1874, believing that Colorado would be healthier than Missouri. He became a professor at Colorado College in 1875. In addition to his teaching, he was involved in mining, metallurgy, surveying, lawmaking, and railroad building, with some of his projects taking him to Central and South America. Until he died in 1919, Kerr kept an extensive stack of personal papers, which are now housed in a special collection at Colorado College.

After Kerr's departure, the Fruitland Normal Institute seems to have continued for a short time but then disappeared from the historical record. The State Commissioner of Education reported that the institute was an active normal school in 1875 with a library containing 1,000 volumes. However, I haven't been able to find any references to the school past that.

According to Dr. Nickell, the village of Fruitland was platted by Elam Templeton. This was likely the older part of the town located near the intersection of modern-day Highway 61 and Route FF.

The Fruitland name apparently didn't stick at first, with maps from the 1870s and 1880s continuing to show the area as Pleasant Hill. It wasn't until the Fruitland post office was established in 1886 that mapmakers started to drop Pleasant Hill in favor of Fruitland.

Fruitland received a boost in 1905 when Louis Houck brought his Cape Girardeau Northern Railroad through the village, a way point on the line between Cape Girardeau, Perryville, and beyond. The C.G.N., however, was a money-losing albatross, and service through Fruitland was suspended in 1919. The tracks were removed in the 1920s just as Fruitland was chosen as the route for a new state highway (Missouri 25, now U.S. 61).

Of course, the biggest boost came in the 1960s and 1970s with the opening of Interstate 55 and an interchange at Fruitland.

The opening of a large manufacturing plant near Neely's Landing in August 1969 was also a huge plus, as many of the workers settled in the Fruitland area.

Even with its favorable location and growth over the years, Fruitland has resisted forming its own government in the past. A soil survey map from 1912 shows Fruitland surrounded by a dotted line, suggesting that the town was incorporated, but I haven't been able to find any evidence that Fruitland ever did so.

Now that Jackson annexed a portion of Fruitland, let's hope that Fruitland's identity and history aren't lost in the shuffle.

Shepherd Mountain

"The Shepherd Mountain ore is perhaps the best iron-ore in Missouri." — *Iron Ores of Missouri and Michigan*, 1876

With names like Iron County, Ironton, Iron Mountain, and Irondale, it's clear that iron mining played a key part in local history. Shepherd Mountain, a large peak rising above the town of Ironton, was one of the first places to be worked by iron miners.

In 1815 or 1816 (sources vary), the first iron furnace was built in Missouri. Located on Stouts Creek just above modern-day Lake Killarney, the furnace used iron ore obtained from Shepherd Mountain and elsewhere.

This furnace was short-lived, but it was a precursor to the coming mining boom. The mining industry prompted the creation of Iron County in 1857 and the construction of the St. Louis & Iron Mountain Railroad in 1858.

Shepherd Mountain produced high-quality iron ore, but most of the deposits were only found at the surface. The miners soon focused their attention on two other peaks, Iron Mountain and Pilot Knob, which promised a larger bonanza of iron ore – although these deposits weren't as abundant as first thought.

Evidence of the mining, including large trenches, can still be seen near the summit of Shepherd Mountain.

The city of Ironton, which owns 840 acres of the mountain, opened a hiking trail during the Summer of 2013.

It's not an easy trek. Starting at the parking lot, hikers are immediately confronted with a choice: Take the steep trail, or take the less steep route.

The "steep" trail goes straight up, rapidly gaining 400 feet in elevation. The "less steep" route also climbs the same distance, but not so quickly.

The reward at the top is a bird's eye view of the town of Pilot Knob...

...as well as the mountain of Pilot Knob.

However, this isn't the summit. That involves another 300 feet elevation gain to reach the high point of 1,608 feet.

The trail passes two obvious mining trenches. A third "diggings" spot can be found off-trail, southwest of the peak.

After leaving the summit, the loop trail meets a large glade on the southeast side of the mountain.

This clearing was one of the locations where Confederate soldiers fired cannon during their ill-fated assault on Fort Davidson in 1864.

Although trees obscure the view now, the cannon emplacement had a commanding view of the fort and Pilot Knob.

The town of Arcadia can also be seen from the glade, including the large Baptist Home building, completed in 1923.

On the way back to the parking lot, the trail encounters another short-lived venture: a ski run. The remains of the ski lift are still visible, although the structures appear quite primitive.

With its Civil War history, the remains of two industries (mining and skiing), and its natural beauty, Shepherd Mountain is quite a gem.

Directions

From Cape Girardeau, take Highway 72 through Patton and Fredericktown to Arcadia. After crossing the viaduct into Arcadia, turn right and then turn left (north) on Highway 21. Just before reaching the town of Pilot Knob, look for the big sign for the

The trail encounters a short-lived ski run on Shepherd Mountain.

Shepherd Mountain Hiking Trail. Turn left into the driveway for a pharmacy (formerly a drive-in restaurant) and then bear right on a gravel drive. This lane leads to the parking lot and trailhead.

The loop trail is 3.5 miles long. While not as strenuous as other nearby trails I've previously described at Buford or Black Mountains, this one is certainly challenging.

SCENIC WONDERS

Pickle Springs

Remember the Road Runner cartoons?

Wile E. Coyote always found himself in the middle of a ridiculous landscape of arches, spires and cliffs that defied gravity.

The headwaters of Pickle Creek spill over a small ledge at Pickle Springs, the namesake of the natural area.

Missouri has something like that, but on a much smaller scale – Pickle Springs Natural Area in Ste. Genevieve County features peculiar rock formations that could easily form the backdrop of a cartoon.

A two-mile trail loops through the natural area, passing curiosities with names like the Keyhole and Terrapin Rock. The trail is a moderate hike and can be done in an hour at a leisurely pace, but will take longer because the natural rock formations and scenery beg to be admired.

Not far from the parking lot, the trail makes a grand entrance through the Slot, a long crevice only a few feet wide.

The gravity-defying Double Arch at Pickle Springs Natural Area features a pair of thin columns that support a rock ledge.

Soon after, the trail encounters Double Arch, arguably the most photographic feature at Pickle Springs. Two slender columns support a rock ledge. This, in turn, supports an elephant-sized boulder standing precariously on two tiny feet. The scene will make you wonder how the formation is still standing.

Around the corner, two rocks lean against each other to form a narrow arch under which the trail passes. This is the Keyhole.

The gravity-defying Double Arch found at Pickle Springs is just one of many wonders here.

On the other side of the passage, a pair of trees has been uprooted and are now resting lazily against a rock.

Next, the trail skirts around a boulder called Terrapin Rock. Terrapin is an old word for turtle, and this rock does, indeed, look like a turtle from a certain angle.

The trail meanders across a series of hills and creeks before reaching Spirit Canyon, a horseshoe-shaped valley lined with rock bluffs. A sandstone shelter along one side is just big enough to provide protection from the rain.

After climbing out of Spirit Canyon, the trail opens suddenly into a clearing, Dome Rock, that provides a panoramic view of the Pickle Creek valley. After hiking for over a mile in dense woods, the view at Dome Rock is unexpected, and it takes a few moments to adjust to the bright sunlight.

Leaving the hills, the trail drops down into the valley and reaches the namesake Pickle Springs, where the headwaters of Pickle Creek trickle across a low waterfall. The creek was reportedly named for William Pickles, an early landowner who was killed during the Civil War.

Finally, the trail enters one more canyon, Rockpile Canyon, filled with a haphazard collection of boulders that have tumbled from the cliffs above. It's hard to resist the temptation to scramble across the rocks for a better look. The rocks are fairly stable. The trail has warning signs to adhere to, but this pile is unmarked.

It's also hard to leave Rockpile Canyon, knowing that the parking lot is only a short distance away. However, a sign at the end of the trail provides driving directions to another nearby natural area, Hickory Canyons, that includes even more rock formations that Wile E. Coyote could call home.

Directions

From Cape Girardeau, take Interstate 55 North to the Highway 32 interchange at Ste. Genevieve (Exit 150). Turn left and take Highway 32 west for 16 miles to the junction with Route AA. Follow AA for three-quarters of a mile and make a sharp left on Dorlac Road. A short distance on this gravel road, look for the Pickle Springs parking area on the right.

Rocky Falls

Our region has many colorful placenames: Elephant Rocks, Stony Battery, Hanging Dog Island, Ghost Dance Canyon, Devils Tollgate, and even Monkeys Eyebrow. Sometimes, however, the best names are the most simple.

Big Spring, for instance, reveals everything you need to know: it's a big spring. It's so big it doesn't need a flowery name.

Rocky Falls in Shannon County is the same way. It's a waterfall over a rocky hillside. It lives up to its simple name.

The appropriately-named Rocky Creek encounters a steep hillside of solid rock, sending the water cascading into a plunge pool below.

It's too steep to be a classic shut-ins, but not steep enough to be a classic waterfall.

Nevertheless, it's no surprise that Rocky Falls is a popular swimmin' hole in the summer.

Above the falls, Rocky Creek travels through a narrow canyon with plenty of boulders along the way.

If you squint your eyes, you can almost pretend this is Colorado or New Mexico. The wild cactus growing here adds to the illusion.

Another shut-ins is reportedly located a couple of miles downstream next to the abandoned Klepzig Mill. Thanks to the hot weather and wildly conflicting driving directions, I decided to give the old mill a pass. However, I did stumble across a beautiful landing along the Current River.

Water cascading into a plunge pool below at Rocky Falls.

Dirt roads and trails seemed to lead in every direction. Topographic maps show some interesting placenames nearby, such as Buttin Rock, Slick Rock Hollow, and Pole Bridge Hollow, all part of the Ozark National Scenic Riverways.

Directions

Rocky Falls is located between Eminence and Van Buren, a good 3+ hour drive from Cape Girardeau.

From Cape, you can either take I-55 to Sikeston and then US 60 to Van Buren (the boring but easy route) or take Highway 34 west through Piedmont to Van Buren (the scenic but difficult route). From Van Buren, follow US 60 west to Winona and make a right on Highway 19 north. Before leaving Winona, turn right on Route H and follow it 8.5 miles to the turnoff for Route NN. Take Route NN east for 2 miles and keep your eyes peeled for the Rocky Falls turnoff on the right. The turn is easy to miss, as it's located at the bottom of a hill and sharp curve.

The driving directions for reaching Klepzig Mill vary between sources. From what I can tell, the best route is to take Route NN to the end of the pavement, and then turn left on the gravel road (County Road NN-522). This road reportedly passes near the mill, but I can't make any guarantees.

Falling Spring

What happens when you combine a spring and a waterfall?

Deep within the Mark Twain National Forest in Oregon County, the water at Falling Spring gushes from the side of a bluff and drops 8-10 feet into a pond.

By itself, the falls would make for a spectacular sight. But Falling Spring also includes a preserved mill and a log cabin.

Falling Spring was homesteaded in 1851 by the Thomas Brown family. They moved from Tennessee, crossing the Mississippi River at "Green's Old Ferry" (present-day Trails of Tears State Park) and continued westward into Oregon County. It's no surprise that they would have chosen this site for their new home. The Brown cabin, with its half-dovetailed log joints, has stood the test of time and remains in good condition, except for some graffiti.

The spring, with an average production of 500,000 gallons per day, was the perfect place for a homestead and mill. The current mill, built in the late 1920s, still has an overshot wheel and some of the interior machinery.

The mill sits immediately next to the spring. Originally, a chute would have connected the spring outlet with the overshot wheel.

In its heyday, the Falling Spring settlement was an important way point on the "Old Thomasville Road" a pioneer road leading from Carter to Oregon counties. Today, this is a remote, and largely undiscovered, recreation area served by a narrow national forest lane that carries very little traffic.

Water and mill found deep within the Mark Twain National Forest.

Located 150 miles from Cape Girardeau, Falling Spring wouldn't be worth the drive by itself. This corner of the Ozarks, however, features plenty to see and do...

Directions

1. Take your favorite route to Van Buren. The fastest route is I-55 south to Sikeston and then west on US 60, but Highway 34 through Marble Hill and Piedmont is more scenic.
2. Follow US 60 west from Van Buren and make a left on Highway 19 South at Winona.
3. Take Highway 19 for ten miles, enjoying the G-forces of the roller-coaster up and down hills along the road, and then keep your eyes peeled for the Falling Spring turnoff (on the left) at Forest Road 3170.
4. Bear left at the fork in the road and take Forest Road 3164 (also marked as County Road 156). Just short of two miles down this road, watch out for the ridiculously sharp turns as the road snakes past the Falling Spring cemetery. The parking area is just ahead on the right.

Greer Spring

In my previous entries, I've described two scenic places in the Mark Twain National Forest west of Van Buren: Falling Spring and Cupola Pond. This area also features another attraction: Greer Spring, the second-largest spring in Missouri.

With an average daily flow of 222 million gallons, Greer Spring is beaten only by Big Spring (286 million) and Mammoth Spring (234 million). However, Mammoth is located on the Arkansas side of the state line (by only 500 feet), so that means Greer Spring reigns as Number Two among Missouri springs.

Water emerges from a cave entrance at the head of a deep ravine and then cascades down a spring branch before entering the Eleven Point River.

Dropping over 60 feet over the course of a mile-and-a-quarter, the spring branch is quite wild. It's too dangerous for boating. For that matter, just walking across the slippery rocks is a nerve-racking experience.

The spring branch provided plenty of power to operate a mill, an opportunity seized by Samuel Greer who built a mill here before the start of the Civil War. The narrow ravine didn't provide any room for expansion, so Greer constructed a new mill in 1899 at the top of a ridge, three-quarters of a mile away. This required building a series of cables to convey power from the spring water. It was a crazy scheme, but it operated successfully until 1920 when the mill became obsolete by cheaper methods of making flour.

Curiously, the spring itself was sold to Cape Girardeau's own Louis Houck in 1904. The Dennig family took over control of

Water cascades down a spring branch at Greer Spring, too fast
to navigate a boat through, just right for admiring from the shore.

the spring and mill property in 1922, using it as a private retreat. An attempt was made by Anheuser-Busch to open a bottling plant here, but public outcry eventually led to the purchase of the spring by the Forest Service in 1993.

As part of the sale, the Dennig family negotiated to retain exclusive rights to the mill for 20 years, so the mill property remained off-limits to the public until 2013. The spring itself, with a one-mile hiking trail from Highway 19, is open to the public during daylight hours.

The information panel at the trailhead describes the history of the mills.

Despite the distance from Cape Girardeau, these three places (Falling Spring, Cupola Pond, and Greer Spring) offer more than enough reasons for a roadtrip.

Directions

Take Highway 60 west from Van Buren to Winona. Make a left on Highway 19 South and follow this roller-coaster road for roughly 18 miles until you see the Greer Spring trailhead on the right. The trailhead is located along the top of the ridge after crossing the Eleven Point River.

Hughes Mountain

Researchers have discovered the oldest known rocks on the Earth's surface. Located along Hudson Bay in Canada, these rocks are only 4.28 billion years young.

Missouri doesn't have rocks quite that old, but the Ozark Mountains are still downright ancient. Our own St. Francois Mountains date to over 1.4 billion years ago, making them much older than the Appalachians (460 million years) and the Rockies (70 million years).

One of the best places to see really, really, really old rocks is at the summit of Hughes Mountain in Washington County, southeast of Potosi.

During the climb to the top, the bald summit doesn't look that special.

But this mountain is unique in Missouri and possibly the entire Midwest. It has columnar-jointed rocks that form vertical pillars with sharp edges. While not very tall, these columns are shaped into hexagons and other geometric shapes, sort of like a honeycomb. In fact, this place is nicknamed the Devil's Honeycomb.

The Devil sure gets around: similar, but much larger, examples of columnar-jointed rocks are found at Devil's Tower in Wyoming and Devil's Postpile in California.

These rocks formed when lava slowly cooled and joints were created at crazy angles, allowing the rock to weather away over time into the pillars.

Devil's Honeycomb isn't confined to just one outcrop but covers a large part of the sprawling Hughes Mountain summit.

The "Devil's Honeycomb" is unique with its columnar-jointed rocks.

With a peak of 1,210 feet, Hughes Mountain is nowhere near as tall as Missouri's highest point, Taum Sauk Mountain at 1,772 feet. But the summit of Taum Sauk is flat – it's really more of a ridge – and the view from the peak is limited.

Hughes Mountain dwarfs the surrounding terrain in all directions, offering a panoramic view.

To the south, the next major peak is Buford Mountain (the bumps in the distance) at 1,740 feet.

The hike to the top is a strenuous, but thankfully short, half-mile climb. You'll want to take plenty of time to fully explore the 1.4 billion-year-old rocks and to enjoy the view of other ancient mountains in the distance.

Directions

From Cape Girardeau, take Highway 72 west through Jackson, Patton, Fredericktown and on to Arcadia. Then take Highway 21 north through Pilot Knob, Belleview, and Caledonia. A couple of miles past Caledonia, turn right on Route M. After 3.4 miles, look for the turnoff on the right for Cedar Creek Road. The parking area for Hughes Mountain Natural Area will be on the left a short distance down this road.

You can also take I-55 north to the Ste. Genevieve exit and then follow Highway 32 west through Farmington, Park Hills, Bismarck, and on to Caledonia. There's a shortcut from Highway 32 by taking Cedar Creek Road before reaching Caledonia, but that involves crossing a deep creek on a tricky low-water bridge.

Lon Sanders Canyon

Wayne County embraces some of the most rugged terrain in Missouri. Mudlick Mountain, at the heart of Sam A. Baker State Park, has such a tall peak compared with the surrounding terrain that some sources claim the mountain can create its own weather.

Clark Mountain is nearly as impressive as it looms over the town of Piedmont. Indeed, Piedmont literally means "At the foot of the mountain."

But this entry isn't about a mountain, it's about the opposite: a deep canyon. Just outside of Piedmont sits Lon Sanders Canyon, a rocky gorge and shut-ins along McKenzie Creek.

Now owned by the Missouri Department of Conservation, the canyon changed hands several times until entrepreneur Lon Sanders of St. Louis tried to build a private resort. Some of the remnants of this defunct venture remain, including stone steps:

...Handrails along a trail overlooking the canyon...

...And a portion of a concrete dam.

The resort idea failed, but the canyon makes for an excellent conservation area with a setting that is surprisingly wild despite its location near a golf course and housing developments. A park like this would be the envy of any small town – or major city.

I visited in October, at the peak of the fall colors.

If you like rocks, water and foliage, Lon Sanders Canyon is hard to beat.

Directions

From Cape Girardeau, take Highway 34 west through Jackson, Marble Hill, Grassy, Silva, Patterson, and on to Piedmont. After entering Piedmont, look for the turnoff for Canyon Road on the right, opposite the Piedmont High School. If you reach the intersection with Highway 49, you've gone too far. Take Canyon Road for a short distance until you see the parking area for Lon Sanders Canyon on the left.

At the parking lot, take the trail on the left, follow it a short distance downhill, and then cross the wooden footbridge on the left. This trail, a remnant of the old resort project, goes straight to the best part of the canyon.

Wayne County embraces some of the most rugged terrain in Missouri, giving hikers a real challenge and excellent scenery.

Mina Sauk Falls

Mina Sauk Falls, in Iron County near Arcadia, is a wee bit easier to visit than it was 75 years ago. The trip no longer involves parking next to a goat herder's cabin and hiking 25 miles through the wilderness, as described in a 1935 Southeast Missourian story.

It's still a challenging hike, though, along a rocky three-mile loop trail. The route starts at the summit of Taum Sauk Mountain, drops down to the falls, and then climbs to the top again.

A sign at the beginning of the trail warns about the difficulty and notes that the waterfall only runs in wet weather. That's the dilemma: in rainy weather, portions of the trail turn into muddy quagmires. So, you want to visit a couple of days after a big rain when the falls are still flowing nicely but the trail isn't a sloshy mess. Good luck!

The trail begins as a paved sidewalk leading to the monument marking the summit of Taum Sauk Mountain, Missouri's highest point. Naturally, it's all downhill from here as the trail turns to gravel and then dirt.

During the descent, the trail passes through three rocky glades where the exposed bedrock has prevented trees from growing. The first glade offers a piece of unnatural art in the form of a precariously balanced cairn.

In between the glades, the trail passes through woods where several thousand boulders and tree roots are waiting for you to trip over. At the third, and largest, of the glades, the mountainside opens up to offer a panoramic view toward the west.

If you squint your eyes, you can see the very top of the new and hopefully improved Taum Sauk Reservoir.

Approaching the falls, the trail squeezes through the mountainside along a narrow rock ledge.

Cascading through a total of 132 feet, the falls are virtually impossible to see all at once. The best view is from the very bottom, which requires following a side trail marked "Devil's Tollgate - 1 mi." It's a steep drop to the bottom along a switchback, but the view is well worth the extra effort.

When I visited, Mina Sauk Falls had a decent flow but was not as spectacular as shown in the tourism brochures.

I did have the good fortune of visiting when the sun was at an angle that allowed seeing a rainbow in the falls.

Beyond the falls, the water flows through a massive field of boulders.

I decided not to tackle the extra two-mile hike to the Devil's Tollgate, a place where the trail slides through a narrow crack between two towering rock monoliths. I was already apprehensive about the climb back to the top of Taum Sauk.

Returning to the main trail, it's possible to walk along the top ledge of the falls. The ledge offers a clear view of Wildcat Mountain, but the falls itself is difficult to see.

Continuing uphill, the trail passes a series of mini-falls and pools along the creek.

From here, the trail veers away from the stream and begins a steep ascent through another glade.

The trail runs parallel to the stream for a distance before turning at an intersection back toward the summit and trailhead. Of course, a visit to Taum Sauk Mountain wouldn't be complete without climbing the nearby fire tower.

Mina Sauk Falls shown with a good-luck rainbow.

Directions

From Cape Girardeau, take Highway 72 west through Jackson, Patton, and Fredericktown to Arcadia. At Arcadia, follow the signs for Highway 72 West and Highway 21 South. This road climbs into the hills and reaches Tip Top Roadside Park. Just after the park, turn right on Route CC and follow it until the pavement ends. Continue straight into the state park and follow the road until it ends at a parking lot for the trailhead.

Johnsons Shut-ins/Scour Trail

What happens after 1.3 billion gallons of water suddenly spill from the top of a mountain? Johnson's Shut-ins State Park has the answer.

Immediately after entering the park, it's obvious that things have changed since that fateful day in December 2005 when the Upper Taum Sauk Reservoir failed.

The park's entrance driveway, moved to a new location, snakes through a field of boulders imported by the wall of water.

To the left, the scour channel created by the flood is clearly visible. It's a chaotic jumble of rocks spanning billions of years of geologic history, rearranged in a matter of minutes.

The park is filled with new roads, trails, picnic shelters, bathrooms, and other facilities. This was clearly a very dollar-intensive restoration project.

Despite the changes throughout the park, one thing has remained constant: the shut-ins.

I can't tell any difference in the chutes, potholes and plunge pools that make the park so popular.

The water is still cold, and the rocks are still slick. On a scale of 1 to 10, with 1 "not slick" and 10 "as slick as snot," the submerged rocks would easily rate a 12.

If you don't want to take the chance of slipping and falling in front of everybody, the area just above the shut-ins provides a nice swimming hole without the potential embarrassment and medical bills.

As in the past, the park only allows a limited number of carloads into the shut-ins area. Thankfully, if you arrive late on a busy summer weekend, all is not lost. The overflow area at the northern end of the park offers the chance to dip your toes in the river and explore the scour channel.

Indeed, the scour channel is so interesting that it could easily form its own state park. The lower section features a slab of bedrock that has been wiped clean. A small creek has started the slow process of eroding new channels in the rock, perhaps creating a "baby shut-ins" in the future.

Climbing upward, the channel makes a right curve, revealing a spectacular glimpse of Taum Sauk Reservoir 2.0.

An overlook on the hillside provides a clearer view of the concrete monolith taking shape.

The overlook includes binoculars to get a close-up view of the location where the water first escaped, cutting a massive gash in the mountain. At the time of the collapse, the side of the mountain probably resembled Niagara Falls and then some.

It's been a long wait, but the restoration of Johnson's Shut-ins is definitely a success – if you're willing to fight the crowds in the summer.

Directions

From Cape Girardeau, take Highway 72 west through Jackson, Patton, Fredericktown, and Arcadia. Follow the signs for Highway 21 north past Ironton and Pilot Knob. Just before reaching Elephant Rocks State Park, make a left on Route N and continue 12 miles to the Johnson's Shut-ins entrance on the left.

Follow the entrance road to the "turnpike" gate. There's no entrance fee, but the park ranger will give you a windshield hangtag so they can keep track of the number of cars that have entered. You can also turn left immediately before the checkpoint to go to the overflow area, which offers a nice view of the boulder field.

Despite changes, one thing has remained constant — the shut-ins.
The boulder fields and cascading water offer a pleasing vista.

From here, you can wade across the river and hike directly into the scour channel.

If you don't want to get wet, the official trailhead for the scour channel is located on Route N, separate from the main park. However, this involves taking a longer hike.

Elephant Rocks

It has been commented that with the arrival of winter, we enter "ugly season."

I disagree. The leaves have fallen off the trees, and daylight is at a premium, but that doesn't mean the outdoors are ugly. If anything, this is the best time of year to go exploring: nuisances such as biting insects, snakes, and weeds are gone. The lack of foliage is a plus, making it possible to see things that are hidden in the summer.

Take, for example, Elephant Rocks State Park. This classic destination looks good in all seasons but is a real treat during a sunny winter day. It's possible to see the "Elephant Herd" from a distance, a view that is usually obstructed by the trees.

"Dumbo" and the other elephants are just as impressive in December as in July.

The record weight for a real African elephant is 12 tons. These Missouri "elephants" are a tad heavier, some tipping the scales at over 600 tons.

Unlike real elephants, there's no danger of getting trampled here, no matter how much you push, pull, or pinch. Scrambling over and under the boulders is a time-honored tradition for visitors of all ages.

Missouri never experienced a gold rush, but the elephant rocks did spawn a "granite rush" in the late 1800s. Just to the east of the modern-day park, the boom town of Graniteville was home to several granite quarries and a rail connection with the Iron Mountain Railroad.

The monument at the top of nearby Taum Sauk Mountain, Missouri's highest point, was made from a red granite slab.

A few years ago, the park added a new trail leading to the "Engine House," a vestige from one of the quarry railroads. The building, not surprisingly built with granite blocks, is mostly intact except for the missing roof.

Some of the original rails can still be found behind the engine house. Starting in 1869, a tremendous quantity of granite blocks was shipped to St. Louis and other Missouri cities for use in houses, public buildings, monuments, bridges, and street paving. It's rare to find a historic building in the Arcadia Valley that isn't built with red blocks.

Leftover chunks of granite can be seen all along the main trail. It's hard to believe that these beautiful blocks were considered rejects. Just imagine what the good stuff looked like.

Everybody wants to take a piece home, but good luck. The park rangers would probably notice somebody struggling to carry a 500-pound rock back to their car.

With smaller crowds, fewer annoyances, and better visibility, Elephants Rocks is a perfect destination for any sunny winter day, if you can catch one. Don't forget about nearby Fort Davidson, Johnson's Shut-ins, Taum Sauk Mountain, Millstream Garden, and Amidon Conservation Area.

Directions

From Cape Girardeau, take Highway 72 west to Arcadia. If you haven't been through Fredericktown lately, watch out for the slightly different routing of Highway 72, now featuring a roundabout.

In Arcadia, Highway 72 crosses an overpass and then comes to a tricky T-junction. Turn right and then turn left to join Highway

Elephant Rocks State Park hosts rocks in the formation of a "herd". These elephants aren't likely to stampede.

21 North. Follow the highway past Ironton and Pilot Knob until reaching the three-way stop with Route N (formerly Route W). Turn left and continue on Highway 21 through Graniteville and to the park entrance on the right.

Hickory Canyons

A "canyon" in Missouri isn't quite as large as a "canyon" in Arizona or Colorado. We don't have anything like the Grand Canyon, but Hickory Canyons in Ste. Genevieve County does feature some surprisingly tall bluffs and rock formations for our corner of the Midwest.

Hickory Canyons Natural Area, managed by the Department of Conservation, is located on either side of Sprott Road, a gravel county road. Driving down the road, you would never know that you are surrounded by steep sandstone canyons.

Two trails lead from the parking area in opposite directions. The short trail on the east side drops into a canyon and ends in front of a waterfall. This is the beginning of Establishment Creek; the curious name comes from an early settlement, or establishment, in the 1790s closer to where the creek empties in the Mississippi River.

Following the creek downstream, many nooks and crannies, including this large side canyon, are waiting to be explored.

The sandstone has eroded into many horizontal ledges. These look tempting at first but are quite narrow and difficult to safely follow.

A spur from the trail leads along the top of the canyon walls to the head of the waterfall. It's a long way down.

The second trail from the parking lot on the west side forms a loop that enters and exits a large canyon formed by Hickory Creek. Traveling counterclockwise, it first descends along a hillside and ravine...

Then crosses Hickory Creek twice...

And passes under some towering rocks…

The best part, however, comes when the trail climbs a wooden staircase past a deep side canyon.

This hollow, surrounded on three sides by ragged bluffs, features many ledges, overhangs, and other assorted curiosities to explore. In wet weather, a trickle of water flows down the rocks.

According to the Missouri Conservation Atlas, Hickory Canyons are the "largest known sandstone canyons in the State of Missouri." They aren't as extensive as the many sandstone canyons in the Shawnee National Forest of Illinois, but Missouri's Hickory Canyons are well worth visiting.

Directions

From Cape Girardeau, take I-55 North to the Highway 32 interchange (Exit 150) near Ste. Genevieve. Take Highway 32 west for 8.5 miles and turn right on Route C. Follow this road a shade over three miles and make a left on Sprott Road. Continue on this gravel road for almost two miles to the Hickory Canyons parking lot on the left. Look for the trailheads on both sides of the road.

Hickory Canyons are the largest known sandstone canyons. Not bad for our corner of the country.

Tywappity Lake

Tywappity Lake was created in the 1950s as a lake for fishing, but the conservation area offers plenty of surprises.

A moderately difficult 2.5-mile trail circles the lake, providing access to all of the nooks, crannies, inlets, and tributaries surrounding the 37-acre lake.

At times, the trail is right next to the water. Sometimes it strays into the woods away from the lake. Elsewhere it meanders around the various tributaries of the lake, crossing the little creeks on wooden bridges.

After crossing a bridge at the far northern edge of the lake, an unmarked side trail branches away from the lake. This rutted trail connects to the adjacent Tywappity Towersite Conservation Area, eventually climbing to the top of a ridge where a fire tower once stood. Just before reaching private property at the crest of the ridge, the trail offers views (in winter) of the flat bottomlands west of Chaffee and Rockview.

I also caught a glimpse of the Emerson Bridge, almost ten miles away to the northeast, but the trees make it difficult to see much without trespassing.

Back at the lake, the main trail continues to offer views of the water from almost every angle.

At one overlook, I spotted a turtle enjoying the sunshine.

Following the trail clockwise, the sandstone creek can be found roughly three-quarters of the way around. It's on the left just before crossing two wooden bridges. If you see tree graffiti that says "JENNIFER WILL YOU MARRY ME", you've missed it.

The trail eventually crosses the dam and returns to the parking lot.

A sign at the trailhead says that the loop can be completed in 1 hour and 15 minutes "at a leisurely pace," which seems about right.

The sign doesn't explain the origin of the peculiar name. Tywappity, sometimes spelled Zewapeta, is the original name for the town of Commerce, as well as a general name for the Mississippi River bottomlands below Commerce.

It's possible that the name shares the same origin as "Tyewhoppety" in Todd County, Kentucky, said to be based on a Shawnee word for "point of no return." This isn't to say that the place is dangerous, but that it marks the halfway point from which it wouldn't make sense to turn back home.

Or something like that. The trouble with Indian placenames is that the first Europeans had a tendency to completely butcher the names, making it hard to figure out the original meaning – if any.

Directions

From Cape Girardeau, take I-55 south to the Scott City exit. Turn right on Route M and drive to Chaffee. At the main intersection in Chaffee, turn left on Route A, cross the railroad tracks, and make two zigzag turns to stay on Route A. Just outside of town, turn left on Route RA. This road ends at the Tywappity Lake parking area.

Tywappity Lake was created in the 1950s as a lake for fishing. There is some debate about its unusual name's origin.

Apple Creek Conservation Area

While hiking at Apple Creek Conservation Area I heard a loud rumbling sound. "That's just a jet," I thought.

Sure enough, the rumbling subsided as a jet airplane flew overhead.

But then a few minutes later, I heard another rumbling sound. "That's just another jet," I thought nervously while noticing that the clouds had started to get rather thick.

No such luck. The rumbles didn't go away. It was obvious that a thunderstorm was approaching.

Naturally, I found myself at the worst possible place along the trail – the halfway point – with the trailhead over a mile away. To make matters worse, two steep hills stood in my way, so sprinting back to the trailhead wasn't an option. At least, not if I wanted to avoid a heart attack, which would definitely put me behind schedule.

After examining the wind speed and direction, estimating the distance from the thunderstorm, and studying the trail map, I could only reach one conclusion: I was going to get wet.

As it turns out, the rain held off until I reached the trailhead. Nevertheless, my prediction was right: I did get wet. Not from rain, but from sweating while frantically hiking the rest of the trail.

This could be a new exercise fad: Thunderhiking. Burn calories while you try to outrun downpours, tornadoes, and golf ball-sized hail! Set new personal records while sprinting across open fields as you dodge lightning strikes! Use new muscle groups while racing up and down steep slopes so you can safely cross that creek ahead before the flash-flooding starts!

On second thought, maybe not. I prefer to do my storm chasing from the comfort of my own front porch, not while hiking on a trail in a remote corner of Cape Girardeau County, where the roads are indistinguishable from creeks.

I guess I should write something about the trail. Apple Creek Conservation Area is best known for its shooting range, yet the multi-use trail provides a quality outing for hikers, horseback riders, and mountain bikers. (But only during storm-free days.)

The entire trail, forming two loops, is 5.7 miles long. Thanks to the ugly weather, I only completed the lower loop. Two trailheads are provided: one for equestrians (at the upper loop) and one for everybody else (in between the two loops).

From the second trailhead, the route follows an old gravel road as it skirts past the shooting range. The well-marked trail eventually veers right and descends into a wide valley along a tributary of Lovejoy Creek. The Conservation Department has planted crops in the bottomlands to provide food for wildlife.

After fording the creek twice, the trail turns right to enter another valley.

Passing a series of plowed fields that have been shoehorned into the narrow hollow, the trail climbs a steep hill to reach a grassy clearing at the ridgetop. It then drops back down over an extremely steep slope.

At the bottom, I spotted a cluster of interesting rock formations along the creek. If the creek had water full-time (it doesn't), these rocks could be described as a shut-ins.

Passing another series of cornfields, the trail ascends a steep hill and then returns to the trailhead. (Actually, the hill wasn't that steep, it just seemed that way when the thunderstorm was only minutes away.)

Hiking along the Apple Creek Conservation Area 5.7 mile trail. Two loops allow for horses and humans alike to enjoy the area.

Directions

Apple Creek Conservation Area is a short 25-mile drive from Cape Girardeau.

Take Interstate 55 to the Fruitland exit (#105). Turn right on US 61 and continue north 3 miles to the turnoff for Route C. Turn right and take Route C north for 6 miles to New Wells. Turn right to stay on Route C, then turn right on Route CC. After 1 mile, turn right on County Road 525. Go 1.2 miles and turn left at the turnoff marked "HORSE TRAILER PARKING." Drive past the equestrian parking area and continue on the access road (making a right turn) until the road ends at the parking lot and gate. Trail maps are provided at the gate, or you can print your own.

Maintz Wildlife Preserve

Once, I found a sunflower patch at Apple Creek Conservation Area.

However, I found an even better display of sunflowers at Maintz Wildlife Preserve, a conservation area north of Millersville also in Cape Girardeau County.

Slightly past their prime, the flowers were starting to droop when I visited in August. They still offered plenty of color...

The Conservation Department plants sunflowers to provide food for birds, especially doves, but also quail, pheasants, turkeys, and others. It's a very effective food source, as five pounds of planted seed can produce over 800 pounds of food.

I would call this a bee-utiful sight, but I hate it when B-level writers buzz their readers with bee-related puns.

The sunflower patch occupies the top of a hillside, visible from a long distance away. I waited for the sun to come out, but some crazy cool August weather wouldn't allow it.

Several doves hanging out at the sunflower field weren't too happy when I arrived. A deer in a nearby field wasn't too thrilled either and made grunting sounds while staring daggers at me before she started bounding away.

In addition to the sea of yellow, this part of Maintz Preserve also includes a stocked four-acre pond...

...plus a classic barn next to a corn field with stalks rapidly approaching the height of an elephant's eye...

...and hillsides chock full of wild plants...

You might be able to catch the sunflowers during the summer before they all slump over and lose their color. Even without the sunflowers, however, Maintz Wildlife Preserve offers a nice place to do some hiking and maybe a little fishin'.

Directions

From Cape Girardeau, take Highway 72 through Jackson toward Millersville. Just before reaching Millersville, turn right on Route B. After two miles, turn left on Route BB near the water tower. Go one mile and look for County Road 471 on the right. Follow CR 471, a gravel road, north for 1.3 miles and look for the second parking area on the left. This lot is signed as Parking Lot #4.

At the parking area, walk past the gate and follow the gravel access road to the top of the hill. When the road curves right to reach the barn, turn left and follow a trail down to the pond. Cross the levee and continue straight through the next field to reach the sunflower patch at the top of the hill.

Note: It appears that the crops are rotated each year, so the sunflowers might be planted at a different location each season. Maintz has 127 acres of cropland scattered throughout 804 acres of public land, so finding the sunflowers (if any) may require some exploring.

A stunning sunflower patch occupies the top of a hillside in Apple Creek.

Red Rock Landing

One winter, I found a population of armadillos at Seventy-Six Conservation Area in Perry County. The little varmints were out in the open trying to find food during the harsh winter.

Another winter, I found a hungry armadillo at Red Rock Landing Conservation Area, just up the river from Seventy-Six. While the climate in Missouri isn't very favorable for armadillos, they seem to be thriving in Perry County, perhaps taking advantage of the many sinkholes to find warm shelter.

The darn things are just so cute, rummaging through the brush for food and standing on their hind legs when they sense danger. They soon forget about the danger, though, and go back to foraging, completely oblivious to everything.

Red Rock Landing offers more than just the chance to see 'dillos. The conservation area has hiking trails, fishing access, and panoramic views of the Mississippi River. The only thing I didn't find was, strangely enough, red rocks.

From the parking area, a muddy trail leads across the railroad tracks and to the river's edge.

The best river views, however, can be found by climbing into the hills. To the north, the Mississippi makes a sweeping curve.

Off to the left, the flat Missouri floodplain stretches to the northwest.

While more difficult to reach, this vantage point is almost as impressive as the overlook at Trail of Tears State Park. And it might include a bonus appearance of an armadillo.

Directions

From Cape Girardeau, take I-55 north to the Fruitland exit (#105) and then turn right on US 61 north. Continue through Fruitland, Old Appleton, and Uniontown. Just before reaching Longtown, turn right on Route D. Then make a left on Route U. At the T-junction with Route C, turn left and drive north to Crosstown.

In the middle of Crosstown, turn right on Perry County Road 350 (it's easy to miss). This road goes 4 miles to the conservation area. The first three miles are paved (barely). Watch out for the low-water crossing of Omete Creek; it's impassable when the Mississippi River reaches 20 feet on the Chester gauge. Follow the road until it ends at the parking area and campsite.

Be sure to print a copy of the area map which shows the hiking trails and property boundaries.

Red Rock Landing offers panoramic views of the Mississippi River and the Illinois shoreline.

Blue Pond

Winter can't last forever. Eventually, the parade of ice and snow storms will be gone, making it safe again to go outdoors.

Blue Pond in Bollinger County is an excellent cure for cabin fever. It has everything for a daytrip: a scenic destination, wildlife activity, and a nice, level hike.

The pond is somewhat of an enigma because it is both a sinkhole and a spring. Sinkholes usually drain water from the surface into a cave system. Blue Pond works in reverse, with a spring at the bottom filling the pond and overflowing into a creek. With an explored depth of 66 feet, it's almost large enough to be called Blue Lake.

It's the deepest natural pond in Missouri and has been designated a State Natural Area.

This setting provides the perfect habitat for beavers. A beaver dam at the lower end of the pond pushes the water level even higher. Still, a fair amount of water flows across the dam into a series of tributaries, with more beaver dams located downstream.

The area below the pond is littered with trees that have been toppled by the beavers. These beavers seem to be more interested in gnawing trees than constructing anything.

Blue Pond is a small part of the sprawling Castor River Conservation Area, featuring many miles of hiking and horseback riding trails. Other trails lead beyond the pond, so there's plenty of opportunity to stretch your legs.

Directions

From Cape Girardeau, take Highway 34 through Jackson and Marble Hill and continue past Grassy. Make a left on Route Y before crossing Castor River. Follow this road until the pavement ends without much warning. Continue straight on County Road 708 for three miles and look for the small sign on the left that says "Natural Area." Take this short lane to the first parking area by the gate.

From Feb. 1 to Mar. 30 and May 15 to Sept. 1, the gate is open and it's possible to continue driving most of the way to the pond. Otherwise, park here and walk along the gravel lane until reaching the second parking lot.

Two trails begin at the second parking area and it's not very obvious which one to take. The trick is to walk past the gate on the right and ford across the creek.

Then bear left, following the wheel ruts across the open field.

The pond is located just beyond the edge of the field. The trail leads directly to the edge of the water and the beaver dam. It's possible to walk all the way around the pond, but the terrain is somewhat treacherous, especially along the right side.

Beavers find a home and build a dam at the Blue Pond. They keep a solid supply of felled trees for their future projects.

Millstream Gardens

Pop quiz: The following photo was taken in which state?

Colorado?

No.

Montana?

No.

West Virginia?

No.

Missouri?

Oh yes.

This is Millstream Gardens along the St. Francis River, between Fredericktown and Arcadia. Here the river cascades down Tiemann Shut-ins in the middle of a huge canyon. During the winter and spring, when the water is high, Millstream Gardens could easily stand in for a mountain stream in Colorado. Later in the year, when the water level drops, the area turns into a serene garden.

Tiemann Shut-ins is a popular place for whitewater rafting and kayaking when the water level is high enough. It's not for the faint of heart...

Rock formations like the "Shark's Fin" lie in wait for inexperienced kayakers.

When I visited once in early April, the river was filled with screaming kayakers. These fools – er, I mean, thrill seekers – could be heard from a long distance away as they barreled down the rapids. It almost sounded like a water ride at Six Flags. This ride, however, is 100% natural and collects no admission charge.

For those preferring solid ground, Millstream Gardens provides a scenic trail that overlooks the river. It starts at a parking area and picnic pavilion above the head of the shut-ins and follows the river downstream.

Don't miss the unusual tree that stands guard over the river below the pavilion.

It's also possible to hike down to the water's edge. The river stage was quite high when I visited, but that's not much of a surprise considering the weather we had at that time.

Millstream Gardens was once part of a private tourist attraction featuring horse-drawn wagons. It's now owned by the Missouri Department of Conservation. A trail connects the conservation area with National Forest land at Silver Mines Recreation Area, located downstream.

If you're looking for Colorado scenery without driving to Colorado, Millstream Gardens provides a cheap alternative.

Directions

From Cape Girardeau, take Highway 72 northwest through Jackson, Patton, Fredericktown. Beyond Fredericktown, continue on Highway 72 for roughly 7 miles and look for a gravel road on the left with the Millstream Gardens Conservation Area sign. Take this road into the conservation area and follow the signs for the River Access/Picnic Pavilion. From the parking area, look for the Trailhead sign and follow the trail as far as you want.

The river cascades down Tiemann Shut-ins at Millstream Gardens.

Logan Mountain Shut-ins

It's hard to beat the excitement of standing in front of a trailhead with absolutely no idea what lies ahead. That was the case when I found myself on a Wayne County backroad riding with a dog who was getting rather anxious and wanted to go for a W-A-L-K.

I happened to find a parking area marked with "Missouri Department of Conservation – Welcome" signs. This was the perfect place to let Shelby the Yellow Dog stretch her legs before she drove me crazy.

She wasted no time pulling me down the trail. It was a boring walk at first through some woods. I knew that the trail probably led down to the St. Francis River, but I didn't look at my maps when I started out from the parking lot (it's more fun that way).

I never did reach the river because, after a short quarter-mile hike, I stumbled across something far more interesting...

It's a rocky shut-ins along a tiny, unnamed tributary of the St. Francis River. The trail actually bypasses the shut-ins, but I heard the distinctive sound of water and knew that I had to explore.

Shelby was quite eager to show off her climbing skills. (She once climbed Tower Rock on her own. Getting her back down was a bit of a challenge, though.)

This is a very "cool" place. I mean that literally, as this is a shady location. In winter, the creek water freezes into curious ice formations.

Oddly enough, the shut-ins empty straight into the floodplain of the St. Francis River (and the upper reaches of Lake Wappapello). It's completely flat just below here.

There's not enough water to make this a swimming hole in the summer. Nevertheless, this small but impressive shut-ins is a "cool" destination in any season. With a convenient parking area just two miles from Highway 34 and a short, easy trail, it's surprising this place isn't better known. It doesn't even appear to have a name.

Directions

From Cape Girardeau, take Highway 34 west through Jackson, Marble Hill, and Silva. Navigate through the crazy intersections with U.S. 67 at Silva and continue on Highway 34 West. Roughly one mile later, keep your eyes peeled for Rebel Cave Road (County Road 310) on the right. This is old Highway 34 and the pavement is terrible. But it doesn't last long, as you will veer right on County Road 311 after only a half mile. This is a decent gravel road. It runs north for one mile and then turns sharply to the left for another half mile. Look for the Conservation Area signs and parking lot on the left as the road enters into the woods. Take the trail for a quarter mile and look for the shut-ins at the bottom of the small valley to the left.

A rock shut-ins finds an unnamed tributary of the St. Francis River — and so do adventurous hikers.

Magnolia Hollow

There are plenty of places along Highway 61 as an alternative to the boring interstate when traveling to St. Louis.

Here's one more: Magnolia Hollow Conservation Area near Bloomsdale in Ste. Genevieve County. Featuring a scenic overlook of the Mississippi River and a large swath of Illinois, this conservation area makes for a nice getaway from the orange barrels and truck traffic along I-55.

Near the overlook is the confluence of the Mississippi with Establishment Creek. The funny name is a corruption of the French word for "settlement," referring to a very early settlement that offered a campsite for those traveling to St. Louis.

Looking downstream offers a view toward Ste. Genevieve and a huge cement plant.

Looking upstream offers a view of the tall bluffs near Prairie du Rocher, Illinois. Almost but not quite visible is Fort de Chartres, a key site in southern Illinois history.

What Missouri overlook would be complete without a Lewis and Clark marker? They passed through here on December 4, 1803.

In addition to the overlook, Magnolia Hollow features trails through the surprisingly rugged river hills. A one-mile loop trail continues past the overlook and down to the mouth of Magnolia Hollow itself. Other trails and service roads snake through the 1,740-acre conservation area.

Forget about the I-55 rest area at Bloomsdale... Magnolia Hollow is a much better place to stretch your legs.

Directions

From Cape Girardeau, take I-55 Exit 154 (Route O) and turn right to reach Highway 61. Make a left, go two miles north, and then turn right on Route V. If coming from St. Louis, take the Bloomsdale exit, turn left to go through town, and then turn right on Highway 61 and drive south to the Route V intersection.

Follow Route V for about a mile and then turn left on White Sands Road. I didn't see any white sands along this road, but it does offer a scenic drive through the Establishment Creek valley. Most of the 5-mile road is paved. Eventually the pavement ends as the road leaves the valley and climbs a steep hill to reach the conservation area. Stop at the last parking area and take the short paved trail to the overlook.

Magnolia Hollow Overlook shown above the Mississippi River. It's a great alternative to boring highway driving.

Cape LaCroix Bluffs

Where can you see Bald Knob Cross, Academic Hall dome, and the towers of the Emerson Bridge all from the same spot?

This isn't a trick question. It's possible to see all three, and more, from a vantage point at Cape LaCroix Bluffs Conservation Area in Scott County.

Sitting at the top of a bluff overlooking the lowlands south of Cape Girardeau, this conservation area offers the chance to see the town from a different angle.

The distinctive dome of Academic Hall rises above the trees in the distance.

Hirsch Tower (KFVS building) is visible behind the cable stays of the Bill Emerson Memorial Bridge.

To the northwest, the cement plant is another obvious landmark on the horizon.

The bend in the Mississippi River just south of town, including the much-discussed wastewater treatment plant, can also be glimpsed through the trees.

All of this pales in comparison, however, to the view of Bald Knob Cross.

According to Google Maps, the crow-flies distance to the cross is a whopping 23 miles. If you were a crow flying between the two places, it would require crossing the Mississippi River multiple times.

While the view by itself is worth the hike, the conservation area offers another attraction... It's the home to a pair of natural arches. Yes, that's right, Scott County has natural arches.

The limestone bluffs have eroded, leaving two large slots in the rock. It's possible to walk through the lower arch.

The broken line of bluffs continue in both directions, separating a high, forested ridge to the south from the flat lowlands.

Cape LaCroix Creek, part of the boundary between Cape Girardeau and Scott counties, originally flowed through these lowlands. The creek now empties into the Mississippi River almost 2.5 miles to the northwest, although the county boundary remains the same.

Springs at the base of the bluffs are home to the endangered Spring Cavefish. This is the only place where the fish species has been found in Missouri – or west of the Mississippi River, for that matter.

Cape LaCroix Bluffs Conservation Area, including 63 acres, was acquired by the Missouri Department of Conservation in 2006 to protect the habitat of the Spring Cavefish.

The river view and natural arches are just a bonus.

Directions

From Cape Girardeau, take I-55 south to the Airport/Route AB exit (#91). Turn left and follow Route AB (Nash Road) east for 3.5 miles. Look for the big SEMO Port Authority sign and turn left on the first gravel road. Park at the small parking area.

Hiking directions

Follow the trail signs, first crossing the railroad tracks and then turning left. The trail leads up a steep hill to the top of the ridge. The conservation area is located on the other side of the ridge, to the right (the land on the left is privately owned).

Cape LaCroix Bluffs offer plenty of nooks and crannies to explore.

Continue past the high point on the trail and look for a spot where the trail turns left and begins a descent. To see the good stuff, turn right here and enter into the woods. If you go straight through the woods a short distance, you will come to the top of the bluffs and the scenic view.

From here, go left to circle the rim of a small canyon that leads to the lowlands below. Make your way into the canyon and look for the natural arches on the right. The area offers plenty more nooks and crannies to explore, but this is the most interesting spot.

Crane Lake

A dreary winter day with a sharp north wind usually isn't the best time to go hiking. At Crane Lake in Iron County, however, it's a plus.

I was invited to a hike at Crane Lake by a local nature meetup group. After setting out from the trailhead, the blue sky was quickly replaced by a slab of clouds accompanied by brisk winds and falling temperatures.

Just great, I thought. What have I gotten myself into?

Once the group hiked around the lake and reached the dam, we found a silver lining. The north wind was pushing the lake water to crash violently over the spillways.

It's quite a spectacle, something that doesn't happen during tranquil weather.

After catapulting over the dam, the water cascades through a large shut-ins along Crane Pond Creek.

Built on solid bedrock above the shut-ins, this would seem a safe location for a dam. Nevertheless, an earlier version of the dam was breached in 1968. The current structure was built in 1971, creating a 99-acre lake.

Today the lake, dam, and shut-ins are owned by the Mark Twain National Forest. From the parking lot, a segment of the Ozark Trail leads to the shut-ins.

From here, it's possible to scramble down to the shut-ins and carefully tip-toe across the creek, joining a second trail on the opposite side that leads back around the lake to the trailhead.

Another option is to continue past the shut-ins on the Ozark Trail, climbing up and over a steep hill with ankle-crunching boulder fields.

The trail leads to a second, but not quite as picturesque, shut-ins along Crane Pond Creek.

Soon, the Ozark Trail turns left and heads toward Marble Creek Recreation Area. The main Crane Pond Trail bears right and soon reaches a slight obstacle: a ford across the creek.

After a futile search for a better crossing, it was clear that everybody in the group would need to wade across barefoot.

Just great, I thought. What have I gotten myself into?

The rocks were slick, but not quite snot-slick, so everybody made it across safely. I quickly gained feeling in my toes about two days later (just kidding).

Past the ford, the trail bears right and meanders up a hill, passing through a series of glades overlooking the creek valley.

The trail then reaches the shut-ins and dam on the other side.

From here it's an easy hike along the lakeshore back to the trailhead. Winter brings an additional perk when hiking along Crane Lake: the chance to spot a bald eagle. Maybe.

Despite the ugly weather, Crane Lake was still an enjoyable hike, made better by the water show at the dam.

Directions

From Cape Girardeau, take Highway 72 west through Jackson to Fredericktown. Follow Highway 72 around the Fredericktown bypass to the interchange with US 67. Hop on US 67 south, then take the first exit at Route E. Turn right (west) on Route E and go 18 miles. Look for the Crane Lake sign at the intersection with Iron County Road 124. Turn left and follow this gravel road for 2.6 miles. At a four-way intersection next to a cluster of houses,

The water cascades through a large shut-ins along Crane Pond Creek in Iron County.

turn left on Crane Pond Road (not marked). Follow this road 2 miles to the entrance of Crane Pond Recreation Area, then continue straight to reach the parking lot, boat ramp, and trailhead.

Hiking directions

The trail leads directly to the dam and shut-ins. After exploring the shut-ins, you have three choices:

1. Retrace your steps back to the trailhead. This is the best choice if the creek is running high.
2. Carefully cross to the other side of the creek at the shut-ins, then follow the trail along the opposite shore of the lake and back to the trailhead.
3. Continue on the Ozark Trail above the shut-ins, then keep bearing right at all trail intersections to return to the dam on the opposite side. Then follow the trail around the lake. Total distance is about 5 miles.

Buford Mountain

It's not the kind of goal that most people would find very impressive: Climbing to the top of Missouri's third-highest mountain.

And yet No. 3 poses a much greater challenge than Missouri's top two peaks.

The trip to the highest point, Taum Sauk Mountain (1,772 feet), is about as easy as falling off a log. Drive to a parking area and walk a short distance along a concrete trail.

Meanwhile, the second high point, Lead Hill (1,744 feet) in Southwest Missouri, is located just off Highway 60 near Mansfield. The summit is on private property, so there isn't much to see.

That brings us to Buford Mountain in Iron County (1,740 feet). Located in a state conservation area, Buford Mountain doesn't feature any roads or concrete sidewalks. It's a difficult, steep, rocky climb from the trailhead.

The eroded trail winds its way up the mountainside, intersecting an antique stone wall along the way. The wall was most likely built to mark a property boundary.

After more agonizing climbing, the trail finally reaches the summit. Congratulations, you've just conquered Missouri's third-highest peak.

Or maybe not. Much like Taum Sauk Mountain, the summit is rather flat and packed with trees, making it hard to track down the exact high point. Unlike Taum Sauk, however, there isn't a big granite marker to locate the spot. According to topographic maps, the high point is located a short distance to the right (east) of the trail, but good luck finding it.

I've got more bad news. You can't see anything from the summit. To get any kind of panoramic view, you'll need to keep hiking. Buford Mountain is actually a long ridge, punctuated by high points. The first summit, nicknamed Big Buford, is the highest, but also the least interesting.

Back on the trail, the path descends a short distance and then climbs to reach another summit. Here the trail passes through a glade or a clearing produced by an exposure of rocks.

Continuing through the woods, the trail reaches a fork. The left fork follows the backbone of the mountain and eventually reaches another summit called Bald Knob.

While not as tall as Big Buford, the bald knob lives up to its name, offering a tree-free overlook of the valley below.

If you squint your eyes and look into the distance, you can almost pretend this is part of the Blue Ridge Mountains of Virginia.

A large outcrop provides a nice throne for surveying the area below.

Beyond Bald Knob, the trail drops down yet again, passing a small man-made pond.

The trail ascends one more summit before turning right and following a loop back to where the trail forked. It's a difficult trek, however, as the trail descends to the foot of the mountain ridge, crosses a few small streams, and then climbs back to the top again. If you follow the entire loop, you will end up conquering Buford Mountain twice. The total hiking distance is over 10 miles.

I'd suggest hiking to Bald Knob and then turning around and following the ridge trail back. In this case the hiking distance is roughly 6 miles, and you only have to climb the mountain once.

A large outcrop provides a nice throne for surveying the area below, if one is so inclined.

Directions

From Cape Girardeau, take Highway 72 west through Jackson, Patton, and Fredericktown to Arcadia. After the overpass in Arcadia, turn right and then left and follow Highway 21 north through Ironton and Pilot Knob. At the intersection with Route N, turn left to stay on Highway 21. Before reaching Elephant Rock State Park, turn right on Old Highway 21 (County Road 36). Follow this road to the intersection with Route U and turn right. After a short distance on Route U, the access road for Buford Mountain Conservation Area will be on the left.

Footnote

Historically, Buford Mountain was considered the second-highest point in Missouri, but everybody had overlooked Lead Hill.

The argument could be made that Buford is actually No. 4, with Wildcat Mountain (approx. 1,760 feet) taking the second spot. However, Wildcat is usually considered part of Taum Sauk Mountain and not counted as a separate peak.

Van East Mountain

I explained the difficulty in tracking down the origins of place-names such as Fruitland, Marble Hill, and Fredericktown. In some cases, the source of a name is clear, but the spelling is not.

Take some of the mountains in Madison County. Blue Mountain, a 1,361 ft. summit near Silver Mine, has nothing to do with the color, even though it does take on a blue tint when viewed from a distance.

According to a Ramsay Placename Study, it's actually named for the Belew family, local pioneers.

Likewise, Van East Mountain, located across from Blue Mountain, shares a similar history. The name appears to be a misspelling of Van Hees. According to land records, Guillaume Frederic Van Hees purchased some of the mountain's land just prior to the Civil War. Indeed, he acquired a considerable amount of acreage in Madison and Iron counties during the late 1850s.

The Missouri State Archives website has a letter from 1857 recommending that G.F. Van Hees be appointed as notary public for Iron County. With such a peculiar name, I think it's safe to figure this is the same person. He must have been fairly prosperous and connected in the community, putting him in position to have a mountain named for him. It's too bad the mapmakers couldn't spell his name right.

Van East Mountain has taken on a new level of significance with a proposal by the Missouri Wilderness Coalition to designate the mountain as a federally protected Wilderness Area. Most, but not all, of the mountain is part of the Mark Twain National Forest. The proposed wilderness would also include nearby Brown

Mountain, named for another pioneer family and not for the color (at least it's spelled correctly).

It's hard to say whether this wilderness proposal has any chance of advancing through Congress. At any rate, we can enjoy this wild area right now. An unmarked, but easy to follow, trail leads from a county road to the summit. While approaching the top, a series of glades to the left provide an opening in the trees.

The clear spots provide spectacular views to the south toward Kelley and Trackler Mountain. The land in the distance is a patchwork quilt of Forest Service and private holdings.

To the southwest looking into the sun, the mountain ridges fade into the distance. If you squint your eyes, you can pretend this is a part of the Blue Ridge Mountains of Virginia.

The rest of Van East Mountain, a mix of trees and small rock outcrops, seemed fairly mundane. Perhaps the most interesting feature here isn't the mountain, but the creek at the foot of the mountain next to the road. This place is called Weiss Shut-ins.

Rock Creek – very appropriately named – flows through a series of shallow cascades.

I was amused to see that a tree had managed to grow out of a sizable crack in one of the larger rocks.

Weiss Shut-ins isn't nearly as impressive as other Ozark shut-ins, but this picturesque spot, along with the misspelled Van East Mountain, makes for a nice destination.

Directions

From Cape Girardeau, take Highway 72 west through Patton and Fredericktown. Turn left on Route D after going through the deep roadcuts west of Fredericktown. Continue on Route D past Silver Mine Recreation Area. The blacktop Route D will soon become gravel County Road 518. Drive for 1.6 miles until the

Van East Mountain glades provide spectacular views to the south.

road comes to a low-water bridge over Rock Creek. Just before this bridge, park on the right side of the road next to an informal campsite. Weiss Shut-ins is all along the creek here.

Walk across the bridge and look for the beginning of the trail on the right. This trail is unmarked and doesn't appear on the Lake Killarney topographic map, but is fairly obvious as it climbs Van East Mountain. It will swing to the left and then the right before reaching the glades near the highest peak. Leave the trail on the left and explore the glades for the best views.

Distance from the trailhead to the summit is roughly three-quarters of a mile with a change in elevation of 500 feet.

Mudlick Hollow

Mudlick Mountain at Sam A. Baker State Park is easily the most frustrating mountain in Missouri.

It stands high above the surrounding terrain but doesn't offer any panoramic views. Like many Missouri summits, the top is generally flat and covered with tall trees. A fire tower sits at the highest point, providing a tantalizing opportunity to climb above the tree line. But the tower is fenced off with big signs warning against climbing it.

The only view is provided by a narrow clearing along a power line. Like looking through a straw, this right-of-way gives the faintest glimpse of other mountains in the distance. It's just a tease.

With an elevation of 1,313 feet, Mudlick Mountain is not nearly as tall as other Missouri summits, including Taum Sauk Mountain at 1,772 feet. However, Mudlick is one of the more difficult to climb, since the trailhead only has an elevation of approx. 440 feet. That means the trail requires a climb of over 870 feet, a serious ascent by Missouri standards.

To make matters worse, the trail is surrounded by a seemingly endless supply of poison ivy.

After such a challenging hike, the viewless summit is a frustrating let-down. Except for bragging rights, the climb to the top just isn't worth the trouble.

That's not to say that Sam A. Baker State Park isn't worth hiking. The park does feature a quality panoramic view, and it's located only halfway up the mountain, at the first of three hiking shelters.

These stone shelters were constructed as make-work projects during the Great Depression.

After the third shelter, the trail forks, with one branch turning left for the Mudlick Mountain summit and the right fork heading to Mudlick Hollow Shut-ins. While the trail to the shut-ins is also a strenuous gut-buster, the payoff is much better.

All along the hollow, a small creek cascades down an intricate series of rock ledges and pools.

Some of the ledges are tall enough to produce small waterfalls.

The trail crosses the creek four times, providing close-up looks at the scenery.

Unfortunately, the climb out of the hollow involves a 500-foot gain in elevation to reach the shelters again, but just think of this as a "State Park Exercise Program."

Directions

From Cape Girardeau, take Highway 34 west through Marble Hill and Silva. Drive straight through the US 67 interchange and continue to the intersection with Highway 143. Turn right here and continue into the park. At the dining lodge, park in one of the parking areas on either side of the road, and look for the big trailhead sign on the left.

Be sure to pick up a color-coded trail map at the trailhead (a printable map is also available online, but it's not as detailed). The total distance to and from Mudlick Hollow is approx. 5 miles.

The trail to the shut-ins is a gut-buster, but the payoff is worth it.

Lee Bluff

I know what you're thinking about this photo. This scene couldn't possibly come from Missouri. This must be some mountain vista in West Virginia or another place far away.

No, it really is Missouri. The water is the good ole St. Francis River in Madison County, not far from Fredericktown.

Lee Bluff, a 300 foot tall cliff, is the setting for this panoramic view.

The bluff overlooks a sharp bend in the river. It's almost too much to capture, even with a wide-angle camera lens.

From here, St. Francis River continues south, flowing through a series of pools.

Black Mountain (elevation 1,502 ft.) looms in the distance to the northwest. On this particular fall day, the mountain was more red than black. The name actually has nothing to do with the color. According to a Ramsay Placenames File, the mountain was named for a pioneer family.

Other nearby mountains, including Arnett and Marlow, were also named for early landowners. However, I haven't been able to find the origin of Lee Bluff. It's a rather mundane placename for such a spectacular scene, one of the best views in all of Missouri.

Scanning the horizon, not one cell or radio tower is visible. Indeed, except for some ATV tracks along the river's edge, the entire view is devoid of any signs of human activity. That's a rarity for this part of the country.

Because of the remoteness, Lee Bluff is not an easy destination to reach. But it's well worth the effort.

Directions

From Cape Girardeau, take Highway 72 west through Jackson and Patton to Fredericktown. Follow the Highway 72 bypass around Fredericktown. At the roundabout, take the second turn to stay on Highway 72 West. Go straight through the stoplight near Wal-Mart and then turn left for the US 67 south onramp. Follow the freeway a short distance to the next exit for Route E.

Turn right on Route E and drive 5.3 miles to Route O. Turn left on Route O and follow this road for almost 5 miles until the pavement ends. Continue straight on County Road 425. After crossing a low-water bridge, the road forks. Bear right on County Road 408. After driving past a farm, the road becomes narrower and rougher. Some maps show this as Forest Road 2064. Keep going for a quarter-mile beyond the last house and look for an ATV trail on the left. Park on the side of the road where convenient (approx. GPS coordinates are 37.45327, -90.45072).

Hike up the trail a short distance to a junction and campsite. Take the left fork as it quickly climbs the steep hill, meandering around downed trees. Follow the trail to the highest point, then bear right to descend a rocky slope a short distance to the crest of Lee Bluff.

Note: Forest maps show that the bluff itself is private property just outside of the Mark Twain National Forest.

The top of Lee Bluff shares a rare view below.

Castor River Shut-ins

Before the Taum Sauk Reservoir collapse, Johnson's Shut-ins was one of the most popular state parks in Missouri, sometimes requiring long waits at the entrance gate during summer weekends. When the park closed, many people were eager to find an alternative swimming hole for those hot summer days.

The crowds made a beeline for the next best thing, Castor River Shut-ins near Fredericktown. What had been a secluded park quickly became one big party spot during summer weekends.

Johnson's Shut-ins reopened, but Castor River Shut-ins have been discovered, and it's never going to be the same.

When I visited, the parking lot was overflowing and several groups of partygoers were carting around large coolers of adult beverages.

If you like to party, this is definitely the place. If you want to enjoy nature, however, I'd recommend staying away during the summer.

The shut-ins are some of the most spectacular in the state, featuring pink granite rock instead of the usual blue-gray rhyolite seen at Johnson's Shut-ins. Castor River is generally a flat, placid stream, but here it cascades through jumbled granite boulders. Over the years, the river has attempted to erode through the hard granite but has only been able to cut a narrow channel, creating the shut-ins.

It was difficult, but I managed to take some photos of the shut-ins without any raucous partygoers.

The flow isn't quite as good as at Johnson's Shut-ins.

This area is part of Amidon Conservation Area, a large tract of public land that also includes the former sites of two mills (Hahns Mill and Mill Shoals Mill) and part of the old road between Jackson and Fredericktown (now County Road 208).

The entrance sign to the conservation area features a millstone from Hahns Mill.

Directions

These directions follow a somewhat roundabout route, but the roads are well-maintained and well-marked.

1. From Cape, take Highway 72 west into Bollinger County.
2. Turn right on Route HH roughly five miles after Patton Junction.
3. Continue on Route HH for 6 miles until the T-junction with Route J, and then turn left.
4. Stay on Route J for a couple miles and then turn left at the intersection with Route W.
5. Drive on Route W until the pavement ends, and then bear left on County Road 208.
6. While on CR 208, keep your eyes peeled for the Amidon Conservation Area sign and make a left on CR 253.
7. Take CR 253 until you see the parking area on the right. From here, the trail to the shut-ins is an easy one-third-of-a-mile walk.

Note: Some maps show other roads that appear to be shorter. However, two of these, Madison County Road 249 and Forest Road 2145, dead-end at private property and no longer connect. Another, Bollinger County Road 928, requires fording Castor River. Finally, Madison County Road 208 does connect with Highway 72 to the west but requires a sharp right turn from the highway that is easy to miss and doesn't shave off much distance anyway.

A lower pool graces a part of Amidon Conservation Area.

182

Black Mountain

Waterfalls in Missouri are frustrating to visit.

During dry weather, they don't run at all. During wet weather, they are beautiful, but the rocks are slicker than snot.

Black Mountain Falls, just off Route E in Madison County, is a prime example. This little-known destination features a series of plunges, each more spectacular than the last.

Timing is everything here. Visit too soon after a heavy rain, and the falls are treacherous to explore, unless you enjoy sudden collisions with the ground. But wait too long after a rain, and the falls shrivel to just a trickle. The challenge is to find a happy medium.

Black Mountain, part of Mark Twain National Forest, has been proposed as a wilderness area. It doesn't have any trails — marked or otherwise. In many places, it's necessary to step carefully through mazes of boulders.

A short distance upstream, walls encroach on both sides of the stream, creating a narrow canyon.

The rough topography makes following the stream difficult. The best bet is to cross the water multiple times and hope that each stepping stone is firm and not too snot-slick.

Despite the hazards, it's well worth the adventure to reach the "Upper Falls." Here, the canyon gives way to a large clearing featuring the tallest of the Black Mountain cascades.

If enough water is running, the stream forks in two, creating a V-shaped waterfall. The right branch passes under a large overhanging rock.

In drier weather, however, the cliff face is not nearly as impressive.

Above the falls, the stream flows through a wide, nearly flat glade offering clear views to Marlow Mountain in the distance.

A makeshift fire ring sits in the middle of the glade, surrounded by vast swaths of pink rocks.

Continuing upstream, the flat rocks give way to another series of cascades.

Eventually, the cascades come to an end as the creek enters the woods. This point is roughly 400 feet higher in elevation than the lowermost falls. That makes this one of the tallest series of cascades – if not the tallest – in Missouri. Taum Sauk Mountain State Park features the tallest single waterfall in Missouri, but in many ways Black Mountain Falls is the more impressive landmark, weather permitting.

From the top of the cascades, it's possible to follow a pair of overgrown jeep trails to the summit of Black Mountain, the highest point in Madison County. But the falls provide plenty to explore.

Directions

GPS coordinates 37.47141, -90.48014

From Cape Girardeau, take Highway 72 west through Jackson and Patton Junction to Fredericktown. Follow the Highway 72 bypass around Fredericktown, then turn left at the on-ramp for US 67 south. After merging on the freeway, take the first exit for Route E and then turn right. (Note: As an alternative, you can also drive through downtown Fredericktown using the 72 and 67 business loops.)

Drive 11.4 miles west on Route E beyond the interchange. The road threads a needle between the St. Francis River on the

The Black Mountain viewed from the highest point in Madison County.

left and Black Mountain on the right. Look for a spot where the road makes a subtle S-curve and crosses a culvert. The lower falls are visible on the right. Parking is limited here, but a pull-out – with just enough room for two cars – can be found a short distance ahead on the left. If you reach County Road 472, you've gone too far.

Walk to the lower waterfall, which is only a few yards from the Route E pavement, then climb past it on the left side. Keep following the creek, crossing where necessary, until reaching the upper waterfall (which is hard to miss).

Sand Prairie

Sand dunes and cacti in Missouri?

It's not a trick question. Scott County is home to Sand Prairie Conservation Area, a tract of land filled with sand, sand, and more sand.

This part of the state might be nicknamed Swampeast Missouri, but Sand Prairie is anything but swampy.

The parking lot immediately opens into an alien landscape of sand dunes and depressions. Trudging from one sandy area to the next, I pictured myself standing on a golf course laid out by a demented designer who insisted on making everything into a sand trap.

On a windy day, the grasses and plants are jostled around, producing intricate patterns in the sand.

To the east, the sand dunes give way to a flat prairie covered in wild grasses and flowers.

The sand creates an environment where rainwater drains quickly, leaving everything high and dry. It's a quality habitat for prickly-pear cactus.

I've seen cacti at isolated locations in Missouri and Illinois, but Sand Prairie is covered by an impressive number of colonies in a variety of shapes and sizes. Look for them in the grassy area north of the parking lot, but watch your step!

The east side of the conservation area is fronted by County Road 335, a road that has no pavement or gravel – just sand. Flanked by a long line of trees, this road gives the impression that it hasn't changed much since the days of the Model T.

The parking lot immediately opens into an alien, sandy landscape.

Almost everything else has changed, though. It's hard to imagine, but this kind of dry landscape once covered a significant portion of the Missouri Bootheel. Just consider some of the historic placenames found in Swampeast Missouri: East Prairie (still exists), Little Prairie (now Caruthersville), Charles Prairie (now Charleston), and West Prairie (near Malden).

Sand Prairie Conservation Area might first appear as some kind of transplant from Arizona, but it's actually the vestige of a Missouri landscape.

Directions

From Cape Girardeau, take Interstate 55 south to the Benton exit (#80). Turn left on Highway 77 and drive just over 2 miles to the intersection with County Road 333. Make a sharp left on CR 333 (paved) and go north for 2 miles. Look for the small parking area on the right.

Royal Gorge Trail

Iron County is lucky to have some interesting hiking trails. I've written about the Shepherd Mountain Trail, by the City of Ironton. Also, the Missouri Department of Conservation has opened a trail above Royal Gorge at Ketcherside Mountain Conservation Area.

Located next to Highway 21 south of Arcadia, Royal Gorge has long been a popular spot for pulling over and taking a quick look at the shut-ins below.

However, the gorge is quite narrow and rugged, making it difficult to cross the creek and reach the main part of the shut-ins on foot.

That's where the new trail comes in handy. It climbs above the shut-ins on the east, providing dramatic views of the gorge.

An overlook provides a bird's eye view of Highway 21 and its Depression-era stone parapet and retaining wall adjacent to the shut-ins.

A second overlook provides a panoramic view to the south along the Big Creek Valley. To the right is the foot of Hogan Mountain, while Ketcherside Mountain is located to the left.

The hillside above Royal Gorge features outcrops of volcanic rhyolite, rock that is over 1.4 billion years old.

Small glades can be found a short distance uphill from the trail.

One of these glades provides a clear view of Taum Sauk Mountain in the distance.

The scenery alone makes the 2.3-mile hike worthwhile, but there's also a bonus: a walk along an old railroad grade from the 1870s.

The Iron Mountain Railroad had to find a way to cross the tall ridge that separates Big Creek Valley from Arcadia Valley. The solution was a steep and curvy approach to this summit, called Tip Top. It was an appropriate name since this location was the highest point along the line. The rails were so steep (2% grade) that helper locomotives sometimes had to be used to provide enough oomph to push trains through this barrier.

In the late 1940s, Missouri Pacific reconstructed the tracks to make this crossing easier. Instead of going over Tip Top, the new route blasted right through the ridge with a rock cut almost 200 feet deep. After the new tracks were opened, the original route was abandoned.

Today, the hiking trail conveniently follows two short stretches of the old rail grade. The first is a walk through the woods that soon converges on the modern-day Union Pacific tracks. The second is a private road, but signs make it clear that the road is open to hikers. The road doesn't follow the old tracks exactly (it's awfully twisty), but this particular spot is where the tracks started their climb toward Tip Top.

This Iron County hiking trail provides dramatic scenery – and exposes a chapter in local railroad history.

Directions

From Cape Girardeau, take Highway 72 west through Patton, Fredericktown, and on to Arcadia. After crossing the viaduct at Arcadia, make two right turns to reach Highway 21 South. Follow the highway to the summit at Tip Top Roadside Park and then continue as the road descends to the other side. Look for the parking area with the sign Coolbaugh Creek Trailhead on the right. This is a trailhead for the Ozark Trail, but it also serves as the starting point for the Royal Gorge Trail.

A trail climbs above the shut-ins on the east.

Hiking directions

From the parking lot, the trail goes left and quickly crosses Highway 21. It meanders through the creek valley before crossing the creek on stepping stones (might be difficult in wet weather). Continue straight as the trail meets a gravel road. From here the trail climbs the unnamed peak above Royal Gorge. Follow the trail to the first overlook above the gorge and explore. A short distance ahead, the trail reaches another overlook. Later, the trail leaves the hillside and descends to the bottom.

The trail seems to come to a sudden end. This is actually the intersection with the old railroad grade; turn left and follow the path north. Although the trail is generally well-marked, the signs for this particular turn are missing. Follow the old grade until it reaches the modern railroad tracks, then walk parallel to the tracks. A private road veers away to the left; follow this road. Soon the dirt road reaches a gravel road and a gate; follow the gravel road to the left. This road will eventually lead back to the entrance trail, completing the loop.

Audubon Trail

The region between Fredericktown and Perryville is a geographic oddity. Five counties – Ste. Genevieve, Perry, Bollinger, Madison, and St. Francois – converge in this area with weirdly shaped boundaries. The peculiar W-shaped line between Ste. Genevieve and St. Francois County even led to a dispute in 2002.

Driving through the area is confusing. From west to east, State Highway T passes from St. Francois to Ste. Genevieve back to St. Francois and back again to Ste. Genevieve counties before eventually terminating in Perry County.

A portion of Highway T traces the historic route of the Three Notch Road, a historic road used to transport lead from Mine La Motte to the Mississippi River. By following the ridgeline of the hills here, the road was able to cut down on the number of river crossings. This was important because these hills contain the headwaters of four different waterways: Whitewater River, Castor River, Little St. Francis River, and Saline Creek.

The Mark Twain National Forest holds a sizable chunk of acreage at the southern edge of Ste. Genevieve County. The hills here don't appear to have a recognized name, but they are traversed by the Audubon Trail, a project of the Boy Scouts. The trail was named in honor of John J. Audubon, the 19th-century naturalist famous for his bird paintings. He spent a brief period at Ste. Genevieve.

Forming two loops, the trail can be hiked in short segments, or completed as a 12-mile adventure. If you aren't interested in hiking, you can drive through the forest on the scenic Bidwell

Creek Road (also known as Forest Road 2199). This road snakes through a tunnel of trees for several miles.

Starting near the tiny hamlet of Womack, the road passes through farmland before entering the forest. Following a ridge, it offers glimpses of deep valleys on both sides.

The road then descends into the Bidwell Creek valley, clinging to the hillside and featuring retaining walls built with rustic stonework.

At the bottom of the hill, the road fords the creek. This is the main trailhead for the Audubon Trail, although the trail does intersect the road at various other points, allowing hikers to mix and match the segments they want to complete.

The picturesque creek was bracketed by wildflowers when I visited.

If the water isn't too high, walking the creek is a fun way to explore and look for interesting rocks.

After the ford, the road climbs out of the valley and continues to wind through the hills. It eventually reaches private property. Keep your eyes peeled for the historic concrete dam across Coldwater Creek on the left. It's posted against trespassing but can be seen from the road.

Soon the road fords Coldwater Creek before eventually ending at blacktop Route WW.

With its remote location, this secluded corner of Mark Twain National Forest is a fine destination for social distancing whether you feel like hiking – or just enjoying the drive.

Directions

From Cape Girardeau, take Interstate 55 north to the Perryville exit (#129). Turn left, cross over the interstate, and then turn right

The Audubon Trail allows hikers to mix and match segments, depending on how much adventure they are up for.

on the frontage road (Lake Road). Follow the frontage road to the stop sign at Route T and turn left.

Follow Route T west for 21 miles to the hamlet of Womack. A short distance beyond Womack, turn right on Bidwell Creek Road (this turnoff is easy to miss; look for the small "BIDWELL CK" sign). After the turn, you will also see a small marker for Forest Road 2199.

Drive on this gravel road until you reach the creek ford. Up to this point, the road is suitable for all vehicles, but you'll probably want a high-clearance vehicle to tackle the ford. If you feel comfortable in crossing, you can continue along the road, although you will have to cross a second, rougher ford later. Finally, at the end of the road, turn right on Route WW to take you back to Route T.

The National Forest website has a printable brochure with a detailed map of the Audubon Trail.

The Road Not Taken

BY ROBERT FROST
Two roads diverged in a yellow wood,
And sorry I could not travel both
And be one traveler, long I stood
And looked down one as far as I could
To where it bent in the undergrowth;

Then took the other, as just as fair,
And having perhaps the better claim,
Because it was grassy and wanted wear;
Though as for that the passing there
Had worn them really about the same,

And both that morning equally lay
In leaves no step had trodden black.
Oh, I kept the first for another day!
Yet knowing how way leads on to way,
I doubted if I should ever come back.

I shall be telling this with a sigh
Somewhere ages and ages hence:
Two roads diverged in a wood, and I—
I took the one less traveled by,
And that has made all the difference.

WORKS CITED

Though every effort has been made to properly cite each source, access to all original notes is not available. Further information can be found online.

"Artesian Well." *Wikipedia, The Free Encyclopedia*, Wikimedia Foundation, 8 March 2023, en.wikipedia.org/wiki/Artesian_well. Accessed 19 Mar. 2024.

Daily Journal Online, dailyjournalonline.com. Accessed 18 Mar. 2024.

Dunn, Joe P. "Kerr, James Hutchison." *American National Biography*, www.anb.org/display/10.1093/anb/9780198606697.001.0001/ anb-9780198606697-e-1002282. Accessed 19 Mar. 2024.

"From the air: Rural communities of Cape County." *Southeast Missourian*, 18 Oct., 1949, p. 3.

"Girardeans climb Taum Sauk; Discover hidden waterfall." *Southeast Missourian*, 15 July, 1935, p. 1.

"Girardeans inspect highway running east from Charleston." *Southeast Missourian*, 21 May, 1921, p.1.

"Interviews with Frank Nickell." Dates unknown.

"James Edgar Wallace." *Find A Grave*, www.findagrave.com/memorial/38957307/ james-edgar-wallace. Accessed 19 Mar. 2024.

"J. Edgar Wallace, father of Cape man, succumbs." *Southeast Missourian*, 8 Feb. 1937, p. 8.

"John J. Audubon Trl System (and West TH)." *Forest Service*, www.fs.usda.gov/ recarea/mtnf/recarea/?recid=21850. Accessed 18 Mar. 2024.

"Lithium Carbonate." *Wikipedia, The Free Encyclopedia*, Wikimedia Foundation, 26 Feb. 2024, en.wikipedia.org/wiki/Lithium_carbonate. Accessed 19 Mar. 2024.

"Mississippi County concrete roads now being built." *Southeast Missourian*, 26 April, 1920, p.1.

"Notched trees found on district highways relics of older days." *Southeast Missourian*, 20 Dec. 1940, p. 1

Powell, Betty F. *History of Mississippi County, Missouri, Beginning through 1972.* BNL Library Service, 1975.

"Ramsay Place Names File." *RAMSAY PLACE NAMES FILE, 1928-1945 (C2366)*, collections.shsmo.org/manuscripts/columbia/c2366. Accessed 19 Mar. 2024.

Schmidlkofer, C.M., "Fruitland booming since highway expansions." *Southeast Missourian*, 30 April, 2007, p. 1.

Schmidt, Adolf. *Iron Ores of Missouri and Michigan. By Raphael Pumpelly ... T. B. Brooks ... and Adolf Schmidt, Etc. [With Plates.].* British Library, Historical Print Editions, 2011.

James Owen Stanley Baughn
12/30/1980 – 12/06/2020

James Baughn was the webmaster of seMissourian.com and its sister newspapers for 20 years. On the side, he maintained even more sites, including *Bridgehunter.com*, *LandmarkHunter.com*, *TheCapeRock.com*, and Humorix. Baughn passed away in 2020 while doing one of the things he loved most: hiking in Southeast Missouri. This is an archive of his writing about hiking and nature in our area.